Taste of Life, Julie Stafford's first book, was a revolutionary breakthrough in terms of health and cooking. It was based on the Nathan Pritikin guidelines of low-fat, salt-free and sugar-free foods – a diet which cured Julie Stafford's husband of cancer. Now, in *More Taste of Life* these principles provide the basis for an even wider range of imaginative and adventurous recipes. It includes new sections of home cooking by popular request – salads for one, barbecues, Christmas fare, home preserves and many others – and together with its predecessor makes up a comprehensive eating plan for delicious food *and* good health.

Some Reviews of *Taste of Life*:

'Discover the secrets of healthy eating without sacrificing delicious food' WOMAN

'Healthy eating doesn't have to be boring' DAILY EXPRESS

'A lively selection of recipes' WESTERN MAIL

'A refreshing point of view' NEW HEALTH

'Strong on ideas . . . with superb photographs' HEALTH NOW

'The recipes are for healthy, but still delicious, food' BIRMINGHAM EVENING MAIL

'A new approach to a healthy lifestyle' LANCASHIRE EVENING TELEGRAPH

GW00728028

Also by Julie Stafford in Sphere Books:
TASTE OF LIFE

More Taste of Life

Julie Stafford

SPHERE BOOKS LIMITED

Sphere Books Limited,
27 Wrights Lane, London W8 5TZ

First published in Australia in 1985 by
Greenhouse Publications Pty Ltd

Copyright © Julie Stafford, 1985

First published in Great Britain in 1987 by Sphere Books Ltd

Photography by Phil Wymant
Line drawings by Gaston Vanzet

TRADE
MARK

This book is sold subject to the condition that it shall not,
by way of trade or otherwise, be lent, re-sold, hired out
or otherwise circulated without the publisher's prior consent
in any form of binding or cover other than that in which
it is published and without a similar condition including this
condition being imposed on the subsequent purchaser

Set in 10/12 Linotron Ehrhardt

Printed and bound in Great Britain by
Richard Clay Ltd, Bungay, Suffolk

Thank you Glenice for making sense of the notes and for your typing skills. Thank you Mum for being my second pair of hands and for sharing your knowledge. Thank you Ann for sharing your ideas. Thank you to all those people (too many to mention) who were the tasters, and offered recipe names even though we didn't use many of them! You made it lots of fun.

I give this book to you Bruce, Timothy and Cassie, for you are my most precious possessions — and your health is your most precious possession.

the diet

This diet is low in fats, cholesterol, protein (especially animal protein), and highly refined carbohydrates such as sugar. It is high in starches, as part of complex, mostly unrefined carbohydrates, and is basically food in its natural state, eaten raw or cooked, but not overcooked.

Note on measurements: this book uses the American and Commonwealth system of measuring quantities in cups, whereby 1 cup is equivalent to 8 fluid oz. This is slightly smaller than the British Standard cup, which is equivalent to 10 fluid oz.

forewords

Health is our God given birth right.

The three corners to the triangle of Health are the physical, the chemical, and the emotional. As with any triangle, if one parameter is affected or changed, then all three must be affected or changed. Hence, a positive improvement of one can result in an improvement of all, and vice versa.

Julie Stafford has concentrated much needed attention to the ever important chemical-nutritional aspect of health. Through her TASTE OF LIFE recipe books, Julie has managed to present everyday-life menus to us in a form that is not only nutritionally sound, but are also easy to prepare and aesthetically pleasing.

It is apparent that mankind is becoming increasingly more aware that the practitioner's responsibility is only for 'health-care', and that the true onus of 'health' is the individual's responsibility. With this in mind, the attitude of mankind appears to be changing from the idea of getting sick people well, to that of preventing the well from becoming sick. Therefore it is necessary to address the needs of *all* humanity, rather than just the 'symptomatically expressive' individuals unfortunate enough to have a diagnosable disease. Mankind has a much higher health potential to achieve. This can only be achieved when the individual accepts responsibility for the quality of his or her own health.

The human race is made up of individuals. If the individual can improve himself, it is possible for all mankind to improve.

Are you prepared to give up what you are, to become what you can be?

Dr. Wayne R. Jennings
B. App. Sci. (Chiropractic)

Julie's first book TASTE OF LIFE was launched in the Spring of 1983. It is still flying high. Its presentation with colourful photographs gave it immediate appeal – but the proof has been in the eating. It showed how to dine well on a low fat Pritikin-type diet.

A little over 12 months later more people now recognise the connection between diet and degenerative disease. Medical trials have since proved beyond doubt the link between cholesterol and heart attacks. High fat diets seem to be one of the factors leading to cancers of the bowel and breast.

Eating less fat, less salt, less sugar, eating more of the complex carbohydrates found in fresh vegetables, fruits and grains, with due attention to other aspects of lifestyle, is acknowledged to be the best preventive treatment we have to offer. And so marked is the improvement in the quality of life of many people eating this way that regression of degenerative disease is considered an exciting possibility.

Healthy choices are becoming easier. Julie's new book is sure to be another significant contribution in this field. May the results of her efforts be helpful to you, as they have been already for others.

Dr. Eric C. Fairbank
M.B., B.S., F.R.A.C.G.P.

contents

. . . If you have your health, you have everything . . .

Keep your diet within your body's means and remember the following:
1 The value of Time
2 The success of Perseverance
3 The pleasure of Working
4 The dignity of Simplicity
5 The worth of Character
6 The power of Example
7 The influence of Life
8 The obligation of Duty
9 The wisdom of Economy
10 The virtue of Patience
11 The improvement of Talent
12 The joy of Originating

I found these words on the wall of a restaurant in San Francisco, and I thought how wonderful life could be if we all took time to make these simple factors the major factors of our daily lives. Happiness and health surely would result in the harmony of life.

introduction

Since writing *Taste of Life* my love of natural food and my love of cooking and presenting natural food has continued to grow, mainly because of a healthy happy self, a very healthy husband, Bruce, and two very adorable children, Tim and Cassie, who ooze enthusiasm each time they come to the table.

I was recently quoted in a magazine as saying, 'Bruce is so fit he's dangerous'. How true! There are days I find it hard to believe just how sick he really was, and how he suffered from the side effects of conventional chemotherapy and radiation.

The change in our dietary life-style gave us the opportunity to take a positive step in the involvement of our own health. We saw the benefits immediately. After the release of *Taste of Life*, I received a positive response from many people and especially from a caring group of medical persons. They too are now beginning to realize that good health starts with a good dietary life-style – all else falls into place naturally.

In this book I hope you will see the limitless possibilities of using a diet based on a low fat, low protein, low cholesterol, no added sugar, no added salt and high in unrefined fibre foods life-style.

I have included sections in this book like Salads for One, The Barbecue, Christmas Dinner and Home Preserves at your request. Other sections follow on where *Taste of Life* left off. Now that you've acquired the *Taste*, I want you to keep going – but most of all I want you to enjoy it.

The foods I use in abundance are natural fresh fruits and vegetables, grains and herbs. I hope you will enjoy the manner in which I place much importance in the role of the Soup, the Sandwich and the Salad (vegetable and fruit). In the old days these dishes, of course, all took second place to the meat dish. No longer is there need to serve a roast of lamb, beef or pork *with vegetables* or a steak and side salad. The emphasis is on the Soup, Sandwich or Salad to take the centre of the meal table and anything else can merely be a side dish.

Remember that we should eat to survive, giving the body what it needs to be able to work on – not just to indulge and satisfy our taste buds. However, with a little extra thought and effort the eating to survive can be an indulgence in itself.

If you are presently existing on a typical Western world diet, you have already destroyed the capacity of your taste buds to taste the true flavour of food. It has been overpowered with excess fat, salt, sugar, preservatives, caffeine and toxic substances in the food you are eating. You can reverse the cycle by omitting these things from your diet and discovering a natural fresh taste you'll wonder how you survived without.

Health and happiness are a matter of choice – your choice – so make it a wise one!

Good health

ingredients

Grains, grain products

cracked wheat
rolled oats
barley
bran
brown rice
bulghur wheat
rolled wheat flakes
wholemeal pasta (spaghetti, macaroni)
wholemeal plain flour
wholegrain breakfast cereals
wild rice

Legumes

beans (red kidney, lima)
lentils
roasted garbanzo nuts (chick peas)
split peas

Packaged ingredients

apple juice concentrate
cold compressed almond oil (for special occasion recipes and for greasing pans)
eggs (egg whites only)
evaporated skim milk
fruits in natural juices (peaches, pears, apricots)
non-fat or low fat cottage cheese (the fat content in wet cheese should be less than 1 per cent)
low fat grating cheese (fat content should be less than 10 per cent)
low fat liquid milk
non-fat or low fat natural yoghurt
non-fat or low fat ricotta cheese (the fat content in wet cheese should be less than 1 per cent)

natural fruit juices (apple,
orange, mango, apple and pear,
grape, cocktail, tomato)
pure maple syrup (for special
occasion recipes)
soy milk
spreads (for special occasion
recipes)
tomato paste
water chestnuts
water-packed salmon
water-packed tuna
wholemeal filo pastry

Miscellaneous staples

active dry yeast
agar-agar
arrowroot
baking powder
baking soda
carob powder (unsweetened)
cornflour
gelatin
pectin
skim milk powder

Vegetables

all vegetables except olives
avocados in moderation on
special occasions (if using
avocados do not have meat on
the same day)

Fruits

all fruits

Meats, fish and poultry

beef, very lean and ground
chicken (all skin and visible fat
removed)
fish and seafood (low fat
varieties; snapper, sole, bass,
cod or other, lobster, scallops,
prawns)
turkey breasts (all skin and
visible fat removed)
veal (fat free)

Breads

wholemeal, rye, sourdough
varieties, salt free, sugar free
and oil free

Flavourings

capers
flavour extracts (vanilla,
almond), not imitation
mustard (dijon)
vinegar (white wine, cider,
tarragon)
wine: dry white wine for
cooking, and brandy for special
occasions

Herb teas

camomile
lemon
peppermint

Dried fruits, nuts, herbs, spices

dried fruits for cooking
(currants, sultanas, raisins,
dates, apricots)
almonds (for special occasion
recipes)
walnuts (for special occasion
recipes)

basil
balm leaves
bay leaves
caraway
chives
coriander
dill

fennel
garlic
marjoram
mint
oregano
parsley
rosemary
sage
tarragon
thyme

allspice
cayenne
chillies
cinnamon
cloves
coriander
ginger
mustard
nutmeg
paprika
poppy seeds
tumeric

it's common sense

Nathan Pritikin made obvious to me the common sense of what good health was all about, and I thank him for his wisdom and inspiration.

The recipes in this book are adapted to suit Pritikin's Maintenance Diet – not the Regression Diet. (However a lot of the recipes would be suitable on the Pritikin Regression Diet.)

The following is a Table of Foods to use and avoid on the Pritikin Maintenance Diet. You may like to refer to it when planning meals in advance so you do not exceed your limits in certain food areas.

Nathan Pritikin's latest book *The Pritikin Promise* is a must for all persons wanting to know about good health. The Table of Foods to use and avoid is reproduced from *The Pritikin Promise*, published by Bantam Books, pages 162–3.

Table of Foods to Use and to Avoid on the Maintenance Diet

CATEGORY	FOODS TO USE	QUANTITY PERMITTED	FOODS TO AVOID
FATS, OILS	None.		All fats and oils, including butter, margarine, shortening, lard, meat fat, all oils, lecithin (as in vegetable spray).
SUGARS	None.		All extracted sugars, including syrups, molasses, fructose, dextrose, sucrose, and honey.
POULTRY, FISH, SHELLFISH, MEAT, AND SOYBEANS	Chicken, turkey, Cornish game hen, game birds (white meat preferred; remove skin before cooking).	Limit acceptable poultry, fish, and meat to 85/112g per day, maximum 680g per week.	Fatty poultry such as duck, goose.
	Lean fish, lobster, squid, and other shellfish.	Lobster, oysters, clams, scallops, or squid; 100g/day (replaces entire daily allotment of poultry, fish or meat).[1]	Fatty fish such as sardines, fish canned in oil, mackerel.
	Lean meat.	Shrimp or crab, 50g/day (replaces entire daily allotment of poultry, fish, or meat).[1]	Fatty meats such as marbled steaks and pork.
	Soybeans and tofu (soybean curd).	Soybeans and tofu: 100g/day (replaces entire daily allotment of poultry, fish or meat).	Processed meats such as frankfurters and luncheon meats.
			Organ meats: liver, kidneys, hearts, sweetbreads.
			Smoked, charbroiled, or barbecued foods.
EGGS	Egg whites.	7/week max. (Raw: 2/week max.)	Egg yolks. Fish eggs, such as caviar, shad roe.
DAIRY FOODS	Non-fat (skim) milk, non-fat buttermilk (up to 1% fat by weight). (225g = 1 serving)		Cream, half-and-half, whole milk, and low-fat milk or products containing or made from them, such as sour cream, low-fat yoghurt.
	Non-fat yoghurt. (170g = 1 serving)	2 servings/day (on vegetarian days);	Non-dairy substitutes such as creamers, whipped toppings.
	Non-fat (skim) dry milk. 5 tbsps = 1 serving		Cheeses containing over 1% fat by weight.
	Evaporated skim milk. (113g = 1 serving)	1 serving/day (on other days).	

	100% skim-milk cheese, primarily uncreamed cottage cheese such as hoop cheese or dry curd cottage cheese, or cheeses up to 1% fat by weight. (56g = 1 serving) Sapsago (green) cheese.	28–56g/week max.	
BEANS, PEAS	All beans and peas (except soybeans).	Limit to 225g cooked beans on days when fish, poultry, or meat is not eaten. Avoid on other days except for small amounts in salads, or other dishes.	Soybeans and tofu (soybean curd) unless substituted: 100g soybeans or tofu = the poultry, fish, or meat allotment.
NUTS, SEEDS	Chestnuts.	Not limited.	All nuts (except chestnuts). All seeds (except in small quantities for seasoning as with spices).
VEGETABLES	All vegetables except avocados and olives.	Limit vegetables high in oxalic acid, such as spinach, beet leaves, rhubarb, and Swiss chard.	Avocados. Olives.
FRUITS[2]	All fresh fruits	5 servings/day max.	Cooked, canned, or frozen fruit with added sugars.
	Unsweetened cooked, canned, puréed, or frozen fruit.	680g/week max.	Jams, jellies, fruit butters, fruit syrups with added sugars.
	Dried fruit.	28/day max.	Fruit juices with added sugars.
	Unsweetened fruit juices.	113g/day max. (792g/weekly), or	
	Frozen concentrates, unsweetened.	28/day max. (198g/week).	
GRAINS	All whole or lightly milled grains: rice, barley, buckwheat, millet, etc.	Unlimited.	Extracted wheat germ.
	Breads, cereals, crackers, pasta, tortillas, baked goods, and other grain products without added fats, oils, sugars or egg yolks.	Limit refined grains and grain products (i.e., with bran and germ removed) such as white flour, white rice, white pasta, etc.	Grain products made with added fats, oils, sugars, or egg yolks. Bleached white flour; soy flour.

SALT	Salt.[3]	Limit salt intake to 3–4g/day by eliminating table salt and restricting use of high salt or sodium (Na) foods such as soy sauce, pickles, most condiments, prepared sauces, dressings, canned vegetables and MSG (monosodium glutamate).	Salt from all sources in excess of amount permitted.
CONDIMENTS, SALAD DRESSINGS, SAUCES, GRAVIES AND SPREADS	Wines for cooking. Natural flavouring extracts. Products without fats, oils, sugars, or egg yolks.	Dry white wine preferable. Moderate use.	Products containing fats, oils, sugars, or egg yolks such as: mayonnaise, prepared sandwich spreads, prepared gravies and sauces and most seasoning mixes, salad dressings, catsups, pickle relish, chutney.
DESSERTS OR SNACKS	Dessert and snack items without fats, oils, sugars, or egg yolks.	Plain gelatin (unflavoured): 28g per week max.	Desserts and snack items containing fats, oils, sugars or egg yolks such as: most bakery goods, package gelatin desserts and puddings, candy, chocolate, and gum.
BEVERAGES[4]	Mineral water, carbonated water.	Limit varieties with added sodium.	Alcoholic beverages.
	Non-fat (skim) milk or non-fat buttermilk.	See restrictions under DAIRY FOODS above.	Beverages with caffeine such as coffee, tea, cola drinks, cocoa.
	Unsweetened fruit juices.	See restrictions under FRUITS above.	Decaffeinated coffee.
	Vegetable juices.	Not limited.	Beverages with added sweeteners such as soft drinks.
	Herb tea, camomile tea preferred.	2 cups per day.	Diet and other soft drinks with artificial sweetener.

---

1 Our revised recommendations are based on a conservative interpretation of the newest data concerning cholesterol and other possibly atherogenic sterols in shellfish.

2 If triglycerides are above 125mg%, eat only fresh fruit in the permitted amount.

3 Normal salt (sodium) needs are provided by food in their natural state and additional intake should be kept to a minimum.

4 Recommendations on herb tea (other than those given) and coffee substitutes are under study.

egg yolks – what to do with them

Worried about throwing out all those egg yolks? Now you don't have to – and please, your dog and cat do not deserve the high fat and cholesterol diet you are doing so well without.

the egg yolk facial

1 4 egg yolks
   ¼ grated carrot
2 4 egg yolks
   ¼ cup wheatgerm

3 4 egg yolks
   2 tablespoons lemon juice
4 4 egg yolks
   ¼ cup yoghurt (non-fat)

Combine ingredients. Wash face with warm water twice. Wear scarf or shower cap, to keep hair away from your face. Lie down. Place towel over your chest and under chin. Using a pastry brush, apply mixture to face, avoiding eyes, nostrils and mouth. Leave on for at least 20 minutes. Wash off with lukewarm water. Wash again with warm water, then splash face with cold water – a super feeling.

egg yolk hair conditioner

For oily hair
2 egg yolks
¼ cup lemon juice

For dry-normal hair
3 egg yolks
¼ cup water

Wash hair with shampoo and rinse. Combine ingredients. Massage into scalp and to the end of your hair. Rinse twice. Now you have squeaky clean hair!

menu planning –
a week ahead

It is an excellent idea to plan menus ahead. It will help you to shop wisely and avoid waste. But most importantly, it will give you a guideline to follow strictly.

If you plan your meals daily you are more inclined to cut corners or nibble at the wrong foods, while you make up your mind what's for dinner tonight.

The following is just a suggestion, but a good starting point. Once you have mastered the menu planning, change the meals slowly by substituting one meal for another from the book – or if you have my first book *Taste of Life* on your shelf, include some meals from there also.

Some things to remember:
- Only use a meat recipe once per day.
- Try not to have meat on days that you are using recipes with dairy products in them.
- Variety is the key to successful menu planning.
- Eat fresh fruit, soup, wholemeal bread, or cakes/slices (see recipes in this book) in between meals if you are hungry.
- My choice for breakfast each morning is porridge and fresh fruit, but it always makes the day interesting to have a change now and then. Choose your own breakfast selection, keeping the above suggestions in mind.
- Remember, that the following is only a guideline. Adjust recipes where quantities do not suit. However, it is always a good idea to put excess in the freezer, and this will cut down your work load for the weeks ahead.

	Lunch	**Dinner**
Monday	Pastie Vegetable Roll: serve with a Tossed Salad	Turkey Drumsticks: serve with a Tossed Salad *Dessert*: Ginger Pears
Tuesday	Crème of Pumpkin Soup Spinach and Sprouts Salad	White Fish with Lemon Sauce: serve with Baked Potato and a Tossed Salad *Dessert*: Green Goblet
Wednesday	Vegetable Shepherd's Pie *Dessert*: Orange Tang	Lemon Herbed Spinach Spaghetti: serve with Wholemeal Bread Rolls *Dessert*: Pumpkin Dessert Pie
Thursday	Potato Curry Soup Tomato and Sprouts Sandwich *Dessert*: (left over) Pumpkin Dessert Pie	Mushroom Pie *Dessert*: Fresh Fruit Salad
Friday	Quick Spinach and Mushroom Pizza: serve with a Tossed Salad *Dessert*: Apple Snow	Chicken and Carrot Roll *Dessert*: Kiwi Fruit Ice
Saturday	Vegetarian Salad	Filled Baked Butternut Pumpkin *Dessert*: Blueberry Yoghurt Swirl
Sunday	Potato and Pumpkin Layer Pie: serve with wholemeal bread rolls	Tuna Pitas: serve with a Tossed Salad *Dessert*:Pineapple Yoghurt Pie
Monday	Tomato and Rice Slice with Rosemary	Curried Scallops served on wholemeal natural brown rice and wholemeal bread rolls *Dessert*: Pineapple Jellies
Tuesday	Carrot, Leek and Zucchini Soup Chicken and Cabbage Sandwich	Asparagus Soup Selection of Salads *Dessert*: Carrot and Apple Pie
Wednesday	Potted Meat Slices on Wholemeal Bread: serve with Baked Potato and a Tossed Salad	Whole Baked Pumpkin with Sage and Onion Stuffing *Dessert*: Almond Oranges
Thursday	Winter Stock Pot Soup, served with wholemeal bread rolls and a Tossed Salad *Dessert*: Banana Yoghurt Pie	Open Vegetable Pie *Dessert*: Citrus Cantaloup
Friday	It's a Bean Brew Soup Beetroot and Carrot Sandwich	Tuna Potato Roulade *Dessert*: Fresh Fruit Salad
Saturday	(left over) It's a Bean Brew Soup Cucumber Boats Salad *Dessert*: Banana Mousse	Chilled Melon Soup Hot Prawn and Orange Salad *Dessert*: Fresh Strawberries
Sunday	Roast of Turkey Breast: served with baked potato and vegetables	Hearty Vegetable Soup: serve with Wholemeal Bread Rolls *Dessert*: Banana Date Steamed Pudding

herbs

	Flavour	Use
Balm: Lemon	This herb has a very strong lemon scent. The leaves are oval in shape and crinkly like spearmint.	Fresh leaves are floated on top of cool drinks. Delicious chopped into fruit salad. They give a lemon tang to a tossed green salad. Fresh or dried lemon balm may be put into a teapot with tea as a refreshing pick-me-up.
Basil:	Sweet basil has light green, soft leaves. Bush basil has much smaller leaves. When broken and rubbed in the fingers, the foliage has a spicy aroma like cloves. Sweet basil has a slightly stronger perfume than bush basil.	Fresh or dry leaves go into Italian dishes, season tomatoes, eggplant, capsicum, vegetable soups, tomato sauce. The fresh leaves are excellent in a tossed salad, potato salad, rice salad, cucumber, cooked green bean salad. Basil is one of the most useful herbs.
Bay Leaves		A bay leaf is added to a bouquet garni, the other herbs being thyme, marjoram and parsley. It is used to flavour marinades, stocks, soups, poultry and fish dishes and spaghetti sauce. Bay leaves may be used fresh or dried, but should be kept in an airtight container.
Caraway	Frond-like leaves. The pungent seeds are rich in aromatic oils, and are prized for their use in cooking and as an aid to digestion. Store seeds in an airtight container.	Breads, especially rye bread. They flavour soups, stewed and baked fruits such as apples and pears. They flavour vegetables such as cabbage, carrots and cauliflower.
Chives	Onion chives have a round, hollow leaf with a mild flavour of onion. Garlic chives have a flat leaf broader than onion chives and are not such a dark green. The flavour is mildly garlic.	Chopped chives go into salads, cottage cheese and can be used as a garnish for baked potatoes, soups, entrees, fish, sauces.

Coriander	Has lacy, feathery foliage. Ripe coriander seeds are slightly oval, small and a beige colour. It has a spicy aroma.	The ground seeds are used to give a tang to fish, poultry and meat dishes. They flavour cakes, biscuits, pastries and bread. Sprinkle a little ground coriander over apples, pears and peaches while baking. A pinch flavours eggplant and capsicum.
Dill	Has delicate leaves of dark green aromatic foliage. Seeds have a pungently dry aromatic flavour (aniseed). The seeds flavour pickles, chutney, coleslaw, creamed fish, meat loaf, potato salad, cottage cheese, cabbage, cauliflower and cucumber. Dill is an excellent herb used with seafood.	The foliage, either the fresh chopped leaves or the dried crumbled leaves, flavours dips, spreads, sauces, salad dressings, coleslaw, tossed green salads, potato salad, fish and rice. Sprinkle on vegetables lightly.
Fennel	The foliage when fresh is chopped finely and sprinkled over fish while cooking, or the whole leaves are used as a stuffing for fish.	The seeds, which have digestive properties, go into pastries and breads, into fish and meat dishes and can be added to steamed cabbage while cooking. They are excellent in beetroot or potato salads.
Garlic		This pungent herb is used in a tremendous number of dishes, particularly casseroles, salads and sauces.
Marjoram	Oregano and marjoram are closely related herbs.	In pasta and rice dishes, pizza, tomatoes, eggplant, capsicum, zucchini, some meat dishes and savoury sauces.
Mint	A refreshing herb with a cool, clean flavour.	In cool drinks. Excellent with citrus fruits and pineapple, orange and onion salad, new potatoes, peas, carrots, tomato sauces, mint sauce, tomatoes.
Oregano	Has a far more pungent flavour than marjoram.	With pasta, rice, tomatoes, eggplant, capsicums, zucchini, in pizzas and savoury sauces, and also in some meat dishes.
Parsley	A long-time favourite for many reasons. It has attractive leaves useful for garnishes. It has a pleasing taste and contains many health-giving vitamins and minerals. It is also an excellent breath deodorizer after garlic and onions. It combines excellently with chopped chives.	As a garnish or chopped in soups, over salads, vegetables, pasta dishes, rice and mashed potatoes.

Rosemary	The oil in the leaves is very pungent, so use sparingly at first.	Chop leaves fresh or dice, and add them to stuffings for meat or chicken. Add to potato pastry, spinach, carrots, zucchini, eggplant.
Sage	This is one of the ingredients in mixed herbs, the others being marjoram and thyme.	In stuffing with onions. It seasons breadcrumbs for chicken or fish.
Tarragon	A strong flavoured herb, a little goes a long way. The French tarragon is recommended for culinary use. It does not set seeds. Tarragon must be dried quickly to keep its colour and flavour.	The spicy somewhat tart taste of the leaves gives a piquant flavour to poultry and fish. Add to wine vinegar, and keep aside for a dressing.
Thyme	Garden thyme is the kind most used in cooking. Thyme can be picked throughout the year to use fresh in cooking. Thyme is an ingredient in mixed herbs, together with sage and marjoram.	It seasons meat loaf, rissoles, stews, soups and strongly flavoured vegetables like onions, steamed cabbage, swede, turnips and parsnips. Thyme makes an excellent herb tea.

spices

	Flavour	Use
Allspice	A spice which has an aroma similar to a combination of cinnamon, cloves and nutmeg. The flavour is strong, so it should be used sparingly.	To flavour chutneys, relish, marinades, cakes and steamed puddings.
Cayenne	A ground spice of the chilli pepper family.	Sparingly to flavour seafood, sauces, or as an interesting addition to a basic coleslaw.
Chillies	These can come whole dried or finely ground.	To add flavour to curries or chutneys or rice dishes.
Cinnamon	This spice is the bark of a tree native to Ceylon. It is presented in a rolled-up quill form or finely ground. It would possibly be one of the most popular spices.	Adds flavour to rice dishes, curries, cooked fruits such as apples, apricots or pears, cakes and steamed puddings. Cinnamon and orange juice added to a natural yoghurt make a delicious refreshing summer dessert.
Cloves	A spice with a powerful flavour used very sparingly.	Whole cloves or ground cloves are excellent additions when cooking apples and pears, to chutneys, steamed puddings, dried fruits and some vegetable dishes.
Coriander	A spice which comes in seed or ground form. It has an orange-like flavour.	It adds zest to a rice dish or to curries.
Ginger	A spicy warm flavour.	For meat and vegetable dishes it is usually teamed with other spices. For desserts, cakes and steamed puddings it should be used sparingly.
Mustard	Comes in seeds or powder form. Its flavour is pleasantly poignant.	To add flavour to a white sauce, a mayonnaise or vegetable dishes.

Nutmeg	Is most suitably used fresh and grated to capture its true flavour.	A widely used spice in hot or cold drinks, spicy or sweet dishes. Try it with fish, veal, spinach, carrots, cakes and cooked fruits.
Paprika	Spice used for its flavour and colour. It is the ground seed of the sweet pepper and ranges from mild to sweet to mildly hot.	Flavours chicken, vegetables, fish and sauces. Its bright red colour sprinkled over a pale dish immediately adds warmth and interest.
Tumeric	Adds a yellow colour to most dishes.	Use to colour egg whites, rice, or use in dressings, soups and salads.

sprouts

These are a vegetable high in vitamin C, a good source of pure protein; they contain natural carbohydrates, vitamins and minerals. They grow in a jar and reach their desired length (between 1cm–6cm) in 3 to 5 days.

You can buy commercial sprouters but a jar with a piece of muslin secured over the opening is acceptable.

Choose from a wide variety of seeds, beans and lentils available. Sprout one variety or combine two or more varieties for an added interest in texture and flavour.

Soak the seeds, beans and lentils for 6 hours in lukewarm water. Drain. Leave in a light place (not direct sunlight). Rinse sprouts every day and drain well.

Eat them in salads, add to sandwiches, drop them onto soup prior to serving, use them as a garnish or juice them with other fruits and vegetables. They can be added to any cooked meals prior to serving, for example, casseroles, omelettes.

bite size

Bite size recipes can be used for any occasion, but most likely you will use them for special occasions as a pre-dinner nibble or just as nibble food as required.

asparagus roll ups

makes 10

1 cup asparagus purée (Lightly steam fresh asparagus until tender. Drain. Squeeze over lemon juice. Purée and chill)

10 slices wholemeal bread, crusts removed
½ cup non-fat cottage cheese
4 tbsps fresh finely chopped tarragon (optional)

Using a wooden rolling pin roll out slices of bread until they are very thin. Refrigerate for 30 minutes or longer. Push cottage cheese through a fine sieve. Spread bread slices with cottage cheese then with asparagus and sprinkle over tarragon. Roll up and secure with a small toothpick. Repeat to make 10.

Refrigerate for at least 1 hour, remove toothpick before serving.

carrot wheels

makes 24

6 slices of wholemeal bread
½ cup tomato chutney spread, puréed

1½ cups of finely grated carrot

Remove crusts from bread. Using a rolling pin roll out bread as thinly as possible. Lightly spread each piece of bread with tomato chutney spread. Top with grated carrot. Roll up very tightly. Wrap securely in foil. Refrigerate overnight.

Unwrap carefully and cut into 4 wheels (use a very sharp knife or an electric knife). Place on serving platter.

curried eggs

makes 12

6 hard boiled eggs
1 cup cold mashed potato
½ teaspoon tumeric

1 teaspoon curry powder
1 cup cold puréed cooked peas

Shell eggs. Using a sharp knife carefully cut eggs in half and remove egg yolk. Place egg whites on a serving platter. Combine potato, tumeric and curry powder. Mix well. Spoon curried potato mixture into half of the egg white. Spoon puréed pea mixture in the other half. Using the top end of a spoon, just move pea mixture slightly into the potato mixture to create a swirling effect. Chill before serving.

marinated fruit kebabs

This is a refreshing way to start a main meal event on a hot summer's day. Use wooden kebab sticks, approximately 10cm long. Thread on bite size pieces of fruit (about 2 to 4 variations on each stick).

Suggestions:

cantaloup ball, pineapple, apple, orange, honeydew melon ball, green grape, pear, peach, nectarine, watermelon ball, strawberry, purple grape, kiwi fruit, pineapple.

Lie the kebabs in a shallow dish and pour over vinaigrette of your choice. Leave to marinate in the refrigerator until ready to serve. Serve 2 or 3 on a bed of lettuce leaves or cut ½ a grapefruit or melon and stick kebabs into it.

poppy seed log

250g non-fat cottage cheese
1 tbsp finely chopped sage
2 tbsps finely chopped chives

1 tbsp finely chopped parsley
½ cup poppy seeds

Press cottage cheese through a fine sieve, add herbs and form into a log shape. Tear off a sheet of foil, and place poppy seeds on it. Roll the log backwards and forwards through the poppy seeds to coat it thoroughly. Refrigerate for at least 2 hours, wrapped in foil.

Serve with celery sticks, carrot crackers and bunches of green and purple grapes.

prune buttons

makes 24

24 prunes, stoned
¼ cup non-fat cottage cheese
½ cup mashed potato
approximately 10 water chestnuts

¼ teaspoon almond essence (pure extract)
sprigs of fresh dill

Combine cottage cheese, potato, water chestnuts and almond essence in a food processor and blend until smooth. Spoon into a piping bag. Pipe a small amount on each prune. Refrigerate prior to serving. Serve on a platter with a small sprig of dill on top of each prune.

snow pea pods

– a little fiddly, but worth it
approximately 30 snow peas

Filling:

1 cup non-fat cottage cheese
2 tbsps tomato chutney spread
4 king prawns, shelled and finely chopped

2 tbsps chopped chives
½ cup alfalfa sprouts

Wash, string and carefully split the snow peas. Blanch in boiling water for approximately 20 seconds. Remove, and drain. Plunge into chilled water and drain thoroughly. Combine cottage cheese, tomato chutney spread, chopped prawns and chives. Lightly mix. Spoon mixture carefully into the snow pea pods. Press alfalfa sprouts on top of each snow pea pod.

Place on a serving platter, cover and refrigerate for at least 1 hour.

stuffed mushrooms

36 mushrooms
1 cup mashed potato
¼ cup chopped fresh herbs
(oregano, chives, parsley)

¼ cup finely chopped spring onions
2 tbsp finely grated low fat grating
cheese
1 cup wholemeal breadcrumbs

Wash mushrooms thoroughly and remove stems. Combine potato, herbs, spring onions and cheese and mix well. Spoon mixture onto mushrooms and sprinkle over breadcrumbs. Bake in a hot oven 5 to 8 minutes, or place under a hot grill to brown the top.

triangle puffs

makes 16

8 sheets wholemeal filo pastry
1 cup (firmly packed) grated carrot
2 medium potatoes grated and
drained
¼ cup green beans/peas (chop the
beans finely)
¼ cup green capsicum, finely
chopped

½ medium onion diced
½ cup curried sauce (see recipe
curried scallops in Christmas
Dinner section) or 2 teaspoons
fresh ginger juice (press ginger
in a garlic crusher)
1–2 cloves garlic crushed
½ cup non-fat yoghurt
Combine the last 3 ingredients and
mix well

Lay one sheet of pastry on top of each other. Using a sharp knife or scissors cut the pastry as shown to make 4 equal portions. You will need 16 pieces like this. Combine all ingredients and mix thoroughly. To make triangles, place a rectangle of 2 sheets of filo on a flat bench. Fold one corner over to form the first triangle. Open back and place a spoonful of filling as shown.

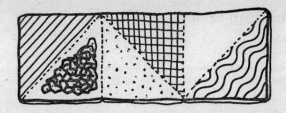

Following the diagram above, fold the shaded area over the filling. Turn this over onto the spotted area. Turn over onto the check area, then onto the white area and finally onto the wavy area. The filling will now be completely concealed. Place on a lightly greased non stick baking tray. Repeat with remaining mixture. Bake at 200°C for 15 minutes. Turn over and cook for a further 15 minutes.

vegetable platter and dips

You will need a serving platter and a selection of suitable vegetables, chosen from the following:

button mushrooms (wash thoroughly)
radishes – halved
green and red capsicum strips
celery – cut into 4cm chunks
carrots – cut in julienne strips or if carrots are large, cut into thin rounds to make crackers
snow peas – top, tail and string
cucumber – peel, cut in half lengthwise and scoop out seeds. Cut into 3cm lengths
cherry tomatoes
cauliflower flowerettes – drop into boiling water for 3 minutes. Drain.
broccoli – plunge into chilled water. Drain.

zucchini strips – drop into boiling water for 1 minute. Drain. Plunge into chilled water. Drain.
Soak cauliflower, broccoli and zucchini in white wine vinegar. Drain prior to serving. Serve with Dips.

avocado dip (a special occasion dip)

Make just prior to serving so the avocado does not discolour.

1 avocado (keep refrigerated until
  needed)
2 teaspoons lemon juice
½–1 cup non-fat cottage cheese
1 tbsp unsweetened orange juice

½–1 teaspoon curry powder or
¼ teaspoon cumin and ¼ teaspoon
  ginger powder
2 tbsps chopped chives

Push cottage cheese through a fine sieve. Remove avocado flesh from
skin and stone. Mash with a fork. Add lemon juice. Combine all
ingredients and mix well.

onion dip

Make just prior to serving

½ cup non-fat cottage cheese
½ cup non-fat yoghurt
1 large odourless onion, finely
  chopped

1 granny smith apple, peeled and
  grated
1 tbsp lemon juice
cayenne pepper to taste

Combine cottage cheese and yoghurt, and fold the onion through. Pour
lemon juice over apple, and add to the onion mixture. Add cayenne
pepper to taste.

spinach dip

1 cup cooked puréed spinach
½–1 cup non-fat cottage cheese
2 teaspoons dijon mustard
¼ cup very finely chopped green
  capsicum

1 tbsp chopped fresh dill
dash of cayenne pepper
1 tbsp non-fat natural yoghurt
  (optional)

Push cottage cheese through a fine sieve. Add all other ingredients and
mix well. If mixture is too dry, add 1 tablespoon of non-fat natural
yoghurt and blend through.

tomato dip

1 cup tomato chutney spread

1 cup cooked apple purée

Combine ingredients.

soups

I look forward to the warmth of winter fires, knowing it is that time of the year for stockpots of soup brewing in my kitchen.

I hardly ever cook the same soup twice – the soup of the day depends on the stock at hand, and what vegetables or fruits are ready to be picked fresh from the garden.

There is enjoyment in a chilled summer soup, on a hot summer's day – but nothing near the pleasures that the warmth of a hot soup on a cold day brings!

Soup is a liquid food, full of goodness made from meat and vegetable stocks and sometimes still containing small amounts of fat free meat, and sometimes all the vegetables. The importance of the soup is that it is all goodness, it is very easily digested and drunk or eaten at any time of the day. In early times, monks in the monasteries would always have a stockpot on the fire for weary travellers.

I have served a soup with the same ingredients more than once, but because the ingredients have been grated, or sometimes finely chopped, or perhaps puréed I have created an entirely different effect and sometimes flavour.

Begin with a basic soup idea, for example, tomato soup; vary one ingredient at a time and then perhaps two to create a different taste result.

Your presentation is also important. It can make a basic soup an artistic and visual delight. Serve soup in pottery mugs for those casual times, in a bowl or serve the soup from the main bowl at the dinner table – an interesting way to create conversation at the table as the bowls circulate with their delightful aromas.

asparagus soup

serves 4–6

3 cups chicken stock
1 cup finely chopped celery leaves
500g (3) potatoes, peeled and
    chopped

350g cooked asparagus
½ cup asparagus cooking liquid
1 tbsp lemon juice

Combine all ingredients and cook for 1 hour. Purée in a food processor until smooth. Serve. Garnish with extra asparagus spears or purée a small amount of extra cooked asparagus and add a couple of tablespoonfuls to each bowl prior to serving and lightly stir through.

beef stock

makes 2 litres

2kg beef bones
1 onion
2 bay leaves
2 stalks celery with leafy tops

1 medium carrot
6 black peppercorns (optional)
2 litres water

Remove all visible fat from beef bones. Put all the above ingredients in a large saucepan. Bring to the boil. Turn heat down to lowest setting. Leave to simmer for at least 3 hours. Remove from heat. Strain. Leave to cool and refrigerate. Remove congealed fat, which will set on top of stock, before using.

Use as required for flavouring soups. This stock can be kept in the refrigerator or frozen.

carrot, leek and zucchini soup

serves 6

4 cups chicken stock
1 cup water
2 leeks, thoroughly washed
3 carrots, peeled

3 zucchini, washed
ground black pepper to taste
    (optional)
2 tbsps parsley

Pour stock and water into a large saucepan and slowly bring to the boil. Turn heat to lowest setting. Remove outer skin and roots from leeks, and cut into 3cm lengths. Cut carrots into 3cm chunks. Cut zucchini into 3cm chunks. Add leeks, carrots, and zucchini and ground black pepper to simmering stock.

Cook for 4 hours. Do not boil again. Add parsley just prior to serving.

celery soup

serves 4

4 cups vegetable or chicken stock
150g chopped leeks
500g celery (preferably leaves and top half of a bunch of celery)
2 potatoes, peeled and chopped

piece of fresh ginger chopped finely
1 tbsp lemon juice
rind of 1 lemon, finely grated
1 cup water
1 cup finely sliced celery

Combine all ingredients (except the cup of finely sliced celery) in a large saucepan. Simmer for 1½ hours. Purée. Return soup to a clean saucepan. Add the cup of finely sliced celery and stir through. Reheat and serve.

chick pea soup

serves 6

1 cup chick peas
250g raw chicken meat (all skin and fat removed)
2 medium onions chopped
1 leek sliced (including the green part)
2 bay leaves
¼ teaspoon thyme

¼ teaspoon marjoram
8 cups chicken stock/water
2 sticks celery chopped (leaves too)
2 large cabbage leaves, finely chopped
1 cup broken wholemeal spaghetti pieces or wholemeal macaroni

Wash chick peas thoroughly. Put into a saucepan with 3 cups of water. Bring to the boil and boil for 2 minutes. Remove from heat and cover. Leave for 1 hour.

Drain chick peas. Add chicken meat, onions, leek, bay leaves, thyme, marjoram and chicken stock. Cover and simmer for 1½ hours. Add celery and cabbage, cover and simmer for about another 30 minutes. Remove chicken meat and cut up very finely, and return to pot. Add the broken spaghetti pieces or macaroni and cook a further 15 to 20 minutes or until tender.

Serve with hot crusty wholemeal bread.

carrot and orange soup

serves 6

12 medium sized baby carrots grated
1 large onion diced
3 cups chicken stock
2 cups orange juice
1 tbsp finely grated orange rind

1 tbsp finely grated lemon rind
ground black pepper to taste
  (optional)
natural non-fat yoghurt and chopped
  chives

Place carrots, onion and chicken stock in a saucepan. Bring to the boil and simmer covered for 20 minutes. Add orange juice, orange and lemon rind, and ground black pepper to taste. Simmer for further 10 minutes and stir occasionally.

This soup can be served hot or cold. Serve with a heaped teaspoon of yoghurt and chives to individual soup bowls.

Variation:

For a thicker soup add 2 potatoes, peeled and cut into small cubes with carrots, onions and chicken stock. Purée the soup in a blender.

chicken stock

makes approximately 1 litre

3kg chicken (meat and bones)
1 piece fresh ginger (approximately
  2 cm piece)

6 black peppercorns (optional)
1 litre water

Remove skin and all visible fat from chicken. Put all the above ingredients in a large saucepan. Bring to the boil. Turn heat down to lowest setting. Leave to simmer for at least 1 hour. Remove from heat. Strain. Leave to cool and refrigerate. Remove congealed fat which will set on top of stock before using.

Use as required for flavouring soups. This stock can be kept in the refrigerator or frozen.

chilled parsnip soup

serves 6

2 medium leeks finely sliced
2 stalks celery finely sliced
4 medium parsnips grated
1 cup fresh peas
4 cups vegetable stock

ground black pepper to taste
  (optional)
1¼ cups skim milk chilled
chopped fresh chives to garnish
2 teaspoons finely grated lemon rind

Cook the leeks and celery in ½ cup of the stock for a few minutes, until all liquid has evaporated. Add grated parsnips, fresh peas and vegetable stock. Season with ground black pepper. Simmer for 40 minutes. Remove from heat. Purée soup in a blender. Chill.

Before serving stir through skim milk and garnish with chopped fresh chives and lemon rind.

chilled summer beet soup

serves 6–8

4 cups puréed cooked beetroot
4 cups beef stock
2–4 tbsps finely chopped garlic
 chives

2 teaspoons finely grated lemon zest
ground black pepper to taste
 (optional)

Combine all ingredients and mix well. Chill. To serve, garnish with a spring onion and grated raw beetroot.

chilled cucumber soup

serves 6–8

1½ cucumbers
2½ cups non-fat yoghurt
2–4 tbsps finely chopped fresh dill

2 cups chicken or vegetable stock
cayenne pepper to garnish

Peel cucumbers and remove seeds. Chop up roughly. Place cucumber, yoghurt, stock and dill into a food processor and blend until smooth. Chill. Pour into individual serving bowls and add a good shake of cayenne pepper.

chilled peppermint soup

serves 4

1 small clove garlic
4 large ripe tomatoes (peeled and
 seeded)
1 large red capsicum, roughly
 chopped
1 large green capsicum, roughly
 chopped

1 medium cucumber
2 tbsps lemon juice
1 cup tomato juice (salt and sugar
 free)
2–4 tbsps finely chopped fresh mint

Place garlic, tomatoes and capsicums in a food processor and blend until smooth. Peel and remove seeds from cucumber and grate. Combine all other ingredients. Chill. Pour into individual serving bowls. Garnish with thin slices of cucumber and a sprig of mint.

chilled yoghurt soup

serves 6–8

5 cups non-fat yoghurt
¼ cup grated carrot
¼ cup finely chopped green
    capsicum
2 tbsps finely chopped chives
    (fresh)
2 tbsps finely chopped parsley
    (fresh)

1 cup skim milk
¼ cup finely chopped celery
¼ cup finely chopped red capsicum
2 tbsps finely chopped basil (fresh)
1 clove garlic, crushed

Blend yoghurt and milk until smooth. Add all other ingredients and mix well. Chill for several hours prior to serving to let the flavours come through. Serve. Garnish with thin slice of lemon.

corn and vegetable chowder

serves 8

3 cloves garlic crushed
2cm piece of fresh ginger finely
    chopped
200g leeks finely chopped
2 cups water
200g celery finely chopped
1 medium parsnip diced
1 large carrot chopped
4 potatoes peeled and cut into small
    cubes

800g pumpkin finely chopped
2 zucchini cut into small rounds
2 corn cobs
10 green French beans cut into 3cm
    lengths
9 cups water
ground black pepper to taste
    (optional)

Cook garlic, ginger and leeks in 2 cups of water in a large saucepan for 10 minutes. Add all other ingredients. Cook on simmer for 2 hours. Remove corn cobs and cut away corn kernels. Return corn kernels to the soup. Stir through. Adjust flavour by adding more ground black pepper if desired.

crème of carrot soup

serves 6–8

3 cups chicken stock
1 cup orange juice
1 leek chopped
1kg baby carrots washed and chopped

1 teaspoon fresh thyme or ¼
  teaspoon dried

Combine all ingredients. Cook over a gentle heat until carrots are quite tender. Remove from heat. Purée in a blender. Return to a clean saucepan and reheat, without boiling.

To serve, add ¼ cup finely chopped parsley and ground black pepper to taste (optional)

or

Serve in individual soup bowls, add a heaped teaspoon of natural non-fat yoghurt, a sprinkle of finely chopped parsley and ground black pepper to taste (optional).

crème of cauliflower and parsnip soup

serves 6–8

175g leeks finely sliced
¼ cup water
200g grated parsnip
400g chopped cauliflower

½ teaspoon nutmeg
ground black pepper
2 litres lamb shank stock

Cook leeks in ¼ cup water until soft. Add all other ingredients and simmer for 1½ hours. Remove from heat. Purée soup. Return to a clean saucepan. Reheat and serve.

crème of pumpkin soup

serves 6–8

1 cup finely chopped leek or onion
2 cloves garlic crushed
1 cup finely chopped celery leaves and
  stalks
2 teaspoons finely chopped ginger or
  2 tbsps dry sherry or ½ teaspoon
  nutmeg
2 medium potatoes, peeled and cubed

1kg peeled and cubed butter-nut
  pumpkin
½ cup unsweetened orange juice
4 cups vegetable/chicken/lamb stock
2 teaspoons finely grated lemon rind
  (optional)

Combine all ingredients in a large saucepan and simmer for 2 hours. Purée soup in a food processor until thick and creamy. Return to a clean saucepan and reheat. Stir through finely grated lemon rind just prior to serving.

curried vegetable soup

serves 6–8

3 cups beef stock
piece of fresh ginger peeled and crushed
1 teaspoon curry powder
200g leeks, roughly chopped

125g parsnip, diced
250g pumpkin, peeled and cubed
1 zucchini, chopped into rounds
400g bottled tomatoes and juice
1 cup water

Combine all ingredients in a large saucepan and simmer for 3 hours. Stir occasionally so vegetables do not stick to the bottom of the saucepan.

fish soup

serves 6–8

2 small leeks (or 2 medium onions if leeks are not available)
2–3 cloves garlic
½ cup unsweetened orange juice
500g ripe tomatoes, skinned, seeds removed and chopped
2 level tbsps tomato paste
freshly ground black pepper (optional)
2 litres fish stock
1 tbsp chopped fresh basil

1 small carrot cut into julienne strips
½ cup leeks (white part only) cut into julienne strips
½ cup celery cut into julienne strips
½ cup fennel cut into julienne strips (optional)
1 kg white fish fillets cut into small strips
8 scallops cleaned
¼ cup finely chopped fresh parsley

Remove the green leaves from leeks and discard. Rinse leeks under running water to remove dirt. Slice leeks thinly.

Add leeks, garlic and orange juice to a pan and cook over a gentle heat for 5 to 10 minutes or until all juice is absorbed. Add tomatoes and tomato paste. Season with black pepper if desired. Cook a further 5 minutes. Add strained fish stock, basil, carrot, leeks, celery and fennel. Bring to the boil and simmer for 10 minutes with lid on. Add fish and simmer for a further 5 minutes with lid on. Add scallops and simmer 4 minutes more.

Serve immediately in a large soup tureen with chopped parsley and hot crispy wholemeal bread.

fish stock

makes 2 litres

1kg clean fish heads or bones
1.5 litres water
500ml apple juice or dry white
  wine
2 large white onions or equivalent
  in leeks

2 carrots, tops removed and peeled
½ cup parsley heads
3 bay leaves
1 sprig of fresh thyme or marjoram
½ lemon

Peel and chop onions. Place all ingredients in a large saucepan and bring to the boil. Simmer for 30 minutes. Strain. Pour strained liquid through a fine piece of cheesecloth (or handkerchief).

Use as required to add flavour to fish based soups or casseroles.

hearty vegetable

serves 8

2 litres lamb stock
250g leeks finely chopped
1 cup chopped celery
1 cup chopped green beans
1 cup shelled peas
2 cups chopped carrot

1 cup chopped zucchini
1 cup chopped parsnip
¼ cup cracked wheat (burghul)
1 cup water
1 teaspoon dried marjoram

Combine all ingredients in a large saucepan. Simmer for 2 hours. Stir occasionally so vegetables do not stick to the bottom of the pan. (This soup is almost a meal.)

it's a bean brew

serves 6–8

2 cups mixed beans (including red
  kidney, split peas, lentils, baby
  lima, garbanzo etc.)
8 cups of stock (of your own
  choice)
1 large leek
2 cloves garlic crushed
½ cup unsweetened orange juice
1 cup fresh chopped tomatoes
  (peeled and seeded)

½ cup chopped celery leaves
½ cup grated parsnip
½ cup grated carrot
½ cup finely chopped parsley
½ teaspoon dried basil
½ teaspoon dried oregano
1 teaspoon dried rosemary
fresh ground black pepper to taste
  (optional)

Rinse and soak the beans overnight or pour boiling water over them to cover, place the lid on and leave for 2 hours. Drain. Split the leek in half and wash thoroughly (white and green part) and chop thinly. Cook leek and garlic in the orange juice over a gentle heat until soft and transparent. Add the tomatoes and cook a further 3 to 4 minutes. Add all the other ingredients and simmer with the lid on for 2 hours or until beans are soft. Stir occasionally, so that beans do not stick to the bottom of the saucepan.

lamb shank stock

makes 3 litres

6 lamb shanks
3 litres water
1 onion
1 cup celery leaves

½ lemon
sprigs of parsley
6 peppercorns (optional)

Place all ingredients in a large saucepan and simmer for 3 hours. Remove from heat. Strain. Set liquid aside to cool and discard the rest. Chill the liquid to congeal the fat. Remove all fat. Use as required in soups and to add flavour to casseroles.

lettuce and alfalfa sprout soup

serves 4

3 cups chicken stock
1 cup apple juice
2 cloves garlic crushed
small piece of ginger crushed
6 green lettuce leaves

1 cup alfalfa sprouts
ground black pepper to taste
    (optional) or a squeeze of lemon
    juice

Simmer the first 4 ingredients in a saucepan for 10 minutes. Tear the lettuce leaves into small pieces. Remove stock from heat. Add lettuce leaves and sprouts. Season with ground black pepper if desired, or lemon juice. Serve immediately.

melon soup

serves 6

4 cups chicken stock
1 teaspoon fresh crushed ginger
1 tbsp dry sherry

1 cantaloup (800g–1kg) peeled,
    seeded and grated

triangle puffs; stuffed mushrooms; marinated fruit kebabs; poppy seed log

fish soup

filled baked butternut pumpkin

salads: cantaloup with prawns; spinach and sprouts salad

rice mould

lemon herbed spinach spaghetti

mushroom pie

juices: grapefruit and orange; tomato spicer; mango and passionfruit

Place the first 3 ingredients in a saucepan and bring to the boil. Turn heat down and gently simmer for 8 minutes. Remove from heat and add cantaloup. Refrigerate. Before serving, adjust flavourings by adding any of the following:

2 teaspoons finely grated lemon or orange rind
2 tbsps finely chopped parsley or mint
2 tbsps finely chopped shallots

potato curry soup

serves 4–6

6 large potatoes
2 leeks
2 medium onions
1/4 cup unsweetened orange juice
6 cups chicken or lamb stock

1 teaspoon curry powder (or more if desired)
1/2 teaspoon ginger
1 bay leaf
3 tbsps chopped parsley

Peel potatoes and cut into cubes. Wash leeks thoroughly and cut both in half lengthwise, chop thinly. Peel and chop onions finely. Cook onions and leeks in the orange juice over a gentle heat, until they are quite soft and transparent. Add potatoes and cook for a further 3 minutes, tossing them through the onions gently.

Add the stock, curry powder, ginger and bay leaf. Cover and simmer for 30 minutes or until potatoes are soft. Stir through parsley before serving.

pumpkin and parsnip soup

serves 8

6 cups chicken stock
4 cups water
1kg finely minced pumpkin (done in a food processor)
200g parsnip finely minced (done in a food processor)
400g celery stalks and leaves finely sliced

ground black pepper to taste (optional)
pinch of nutmeg
2 cups spring onions, chopped, for garnish

Combine all ingredients except garnish in a large saucepan. Bring to the boil. Turn heat down to a simmer. Cook for 2 hours. Stir occasionally.

Before serving, add 2 cups chopped spring onions. Serve immediately.

roast lamb stock

makes approximately 11 cups

3kg lamb shanks and necks
enough water to cover meat in
 saucepan

1 celery head of leaves
3 bay leaves

Place shanks and necks in a roasting pan. Roast in a hot oven 200°C for 1½ hours. Remove meat from pan and place on absorbent paper to remove fat. Place all meat in a large saucepan and cover with water. Add celery and bay leaves. Simmer for 2 hours. Remove from heat and set aside to cool. Refrigerate to congeal fat. Strain through fine cheesecloth and discard meat, bones and fat.

Use stock as desired.

tomato soup

serves 8

1 × 2cm piece of fresh ginger
 crushed
3 cloves garlic crushed
1 large onion or 2 small leeks
1 cup finely chopped celery leaves
¼ cup water

2kg fresh ripe tomatoes peeled,
 seeded and roughly chopped
1 cup orange juice, unsweetened
ground black pepper to taste
 (optional)

In a large saucepan, add ginger, garlic, chopped onion or leeks, and ¼ cup water. Simmer for 8 minutes. Add tomatoes and orange juice, and simmer for 20 minutes. Remove from heat. Purée half the soup, in a blender. Return to saucepan. Season with ground black pepper to taste.

Variations:

- Add 1 cup grated carrot just before serving and stir through.
- Add 1 cup of thin green capsicum strips before serving and stir through.
- Garnish individual bowls with three rings of sliced green and red capsicum.
- Add 1 cup of chopped spring onions before serving and stir through.

tomato and potato soup

serves 6

4 cups beef stock
2 tbsps pure tomato paste
2 teaspoons fresh basil or ½
    teaspoon dried basil
1kg potatoes peeled and finely
    chopped

1kg tomatoes peeled, seeded and
    chopped
1 cup grated carrot
ground black pepper to taste
    (optional)

Stir tomato paste through stock. Add all other ingredients and cook on gentle heat for 1 hour. Stir occasionally. Before serving, stir through 1 cup finely sliced celery and 2 tablespoons of finely chopped parsley.

tomato soup with basil

serves 8

3 cloves garlic crushed
2 medium leeks finely chopped
1 cup finely chopped celery and
    leaves
¼ cup vegetable stock or water
2kg tomatoes peeled, seeded and
    roughly chopped

1 cup vegetable stock
2 tbsps pure tomato paste
2–3 teaspoons fresh finely chopped
    basil or 1 teaspoon dried ground
    black pepper (optional)

In a large saucepan, add garlic, leeks, celery and ¼ cup vegetable stock or water. Simmer for 10 minutes. Add tomatoes and 1 cup of vegetable stock. Simmer for 20 minutes. Add tomato paste, basil and season with ground black pepper to taste. Simmer for a further 10 minutes and serve.

vegetable stock

This is simply any liquid that vegetables have been cooked in. Store in the refrigerator and use as required to add flavour to soups or casseroles.

or

A quick vegetable stock for all uses could be:

1 litre water
1 onion
6 peppercorns (optional)
1 carrot

½ parsnip
½ lemon
a celery stalk with leaves

Simmer for 1 hour. Remove vegetable and other matter. Use as required.

watermelon soup

serves 4

2kg watermelon flesh
2 cups apple juice
1 cup grated apple
1 teaspoon mixed spice (optional)

small piece of fresh ginger crushed
grated rind of 1 lemon
natural non-fat yoghurt

Peel watermelon, remove seeds and chop flesh roughly. Place the first 6 ingredients in a saucepan. Bring to the boil, stirring constantly and gently simmer for 20 minutes. Remove from heat. Press through a strainer into a clean bowl. Chill thoroughly before serving.

Serve in bowls adding a heaped teaspoon of yoghurt and thinly sliced piece of watermelon to garnish.

winter stockpot

serves 6–8

2 cloves garlic crushed
1 large onion cut into rings
2 leeks finely sliced
½ cup of stock (of choice)
2 large potatoes
1 small turnip or swede
2 stalks of celery
½ small cauliflower
4 ripe tomatoes, peeled and seeded
1 cup French beans sliced

½ cup peas
5 cups stock
2 teaspoons mixed fresh herbs or 1
    teaspoon dried
¼ cup cooked wholemeal pasta
    shells or wholemeal rice
1 tbsp finely grated lemon rind
ground black pepper to taste
    (optional)

Cut all vegetables into even bite size pieces. Break cauliflower into flowerettes. Chop tomatoes. Cook garlic, onion and leeks in ½ cup stock until softened. Add potato, turnip or swede, celery, cauliflower, tomatoes, beans, peas and stock.

Simmer for 1½ hours. Add herbs, pasta shells or rice and stir through. Simmer for a further 15 minutes. Season with ground black pepper if desired.

zucchini soup

serves 6

400g grated zucchini
2 onions finely sliced
1 carrot finely chopped
1 potato finely chopped
2 tbsps unsweetened orange juice

3 cups chicken stock
1 tbsp finely chopped fresh
  rosemary
1 tbsp finely chopped chives

Place onions, carrot, potato and orange juice in a large saucepan. Cover and simmer over gentle heat for 5 minutes. Add stock, herbs and stir through the zucchini. Simmer for a further 20 minutes. Purée half the soup and stir through remaining soup. Reheat and serve.

the sandwich

I was amused recently at my dictionary's definition of the sandwich: 'two or more slices of bread with meat or other relish between'. We've certainly come a long way since the Earl of Sandwich (1718–92) named his favourite meal 'the sandwich'! It now comes in many different shapes and sizes, and the fillings are too numerous to mention.

My definition of a sandwich is alternate layers of food on one or more slices of wholemeal bread or rolls. With a little imagination and the use of most vegetables and some fruits, it is possible to see the idea of the sandwich being used not for just morning tea in the shearing shed, nor triangles in the children's lunch box, but as a main course as it rightly deserves.

Adopt a different shape and a different filling for each different occasion: the cubed sandwich for nibbles; the triangles for guests; the rounds for the picnic hamper; the open for a special luncheon; the toasted for supper and not forgetting the Dagwood for when the tummy rumbles!

the open sandwich

Wholemeal bread is an ideal choice for the base of an open sandwich because of the firmness of the bread. Choose from other suitable breads that are salt free, sugar free, oil free, and preservative free (a small amount of sea salt would be permissible), such as ricebread, sourdough, rye, grain, crispbreads etc. An open sandwich is eaten with a knife and fork because the fillings are piled high on the bread. Select ingredients that will compliment each other in flavour and colour.

Some suggestions:

apple and asparagus

On a slice of bread add plenty of lettuce leaves, cooked asparagus spears, slithers of a crisp granny smith apple (add a spoonful of low salt mustard) and finely chopped lemon balm.

apple and celery

On a slice of bread add some shredded endive. In a small bowl, combine 1 red apple cut into cubes, ½ cup chopped celery with 2 tablespoons of non-fat yoghurt, 1 teaspoon cider vinegar and some paprika and mix thoroughly. Spoon over endive. Garnish with cherry tomatoes (4 on a small skewer).

banana and capsicum

On a slice of bread, spread with non-fat or low fat ricotta cheese, top with slices of banana, chopped celery, strips of red capsicum and 2 tablespoons of chopped dried fruit (apricots, dates, sultanas).

beef and water-cress

On a slice of bread, spread with non-fat or low fat cottage cheese (add to it 1 teaspoon of low salt mustard). Top with a thin slice of fat free rare roast beef, finely chopped water-cress and thin slices of cucumber.

beetroot and carrot

On a slice of bread add a large lettuce cup. Line the lettuce cup with slices of orange. Fill with grated raw beetroot and grated carrot. Sprinkle over finely chopped parsley, chives and some finely grated lemon rind. Garnish with red and green capsicum rings.

carrot and fish

On a slice of bread line with very thin slices of low fat grating cheese, some thin strips of carrot, some flaked, steamed, cold fish and thin slithers of green beans. Top with a spoonful of low fat cottage cheese, a squeeze of lemon and garnish with celery sticks and cucumber rings.

celery and tuna

On a slice of bread spread lightly with non-fat or low fat cottage cheese, add a large lettuce cup. Fill with ½ cup salt free well drained tuna, or lightly steamed fresh tuna, slithers of celery and onion rings, squeeze over lemon juice, and sprinkle on chopped fresh lemon balm.

chicken and cabbage

On a slice of bread spread with non-fat or low fat cottage cheese (add to it a squeeze of lemon juice). Top with finely shredded cabbage, some chopped steamed chicken or turkey meat, some segments of cooked apple, a spoonful of non-fat natural yoghurt and a sprinkle of cinnamon.

chicken, nectarine and cherries

On a slice of bread, add some broken lettuce leaves, combine some steamed chicken meat with 2 sliced nectarines, some halved stoned cherries, some chopped celery and some chopped shallots in a bowl. Add 2 tablespoons of dressing and toss. Spread over lettuce leaves.

Sweet Dressing:
⅓ cup non-fat yoghurt
1 tbsp cider vinegar
2 tbsps unsweetened orange juice

¼ teaspoon curry powder
¼ teaspoon ginger powder

Mix all ingredients thoroughly.

egg and potato

On a slice of bread add a large lettuce cup. Fill with cooked potato cubes, the chopped white of 1 boiled egg. Top with a spoonful of non-fat yoghurt to which a dash of curry powder has been added. Add some capers and fresh sprigs of dill.

mint mushrooms and tomato

On a slice of bread, add broken lettuce leaves. Top with slices of tomato and cover with alfalfa sprouts. Combine some sliced mushrooms in a mint dressing and spoon onto sprouts.

Mint Dressing:
⅓ cup non-fat natural yoghurt   1 teaspoon finely chopped fresh
¼ teaspoon garlic powder   mint

Mix all ingredients thoroughly.

orange and corn

On a slice of bread, spread with low fat cottage cheese (add to it herbs of your choice, for example, parsley, chives, thyme or rosemary). Add shredded lettuce, slices of orange (rind and pith removed) and top with cooked corn kernels.

potato, apple and cheese

On a slice of bread spread lightly with low fat cottage cheese, some date and apple chutney. Spread with cooked cubes of potato. Top with slices of a red apple and very thin slices of low fat, salt free grating cheese.

radish and sesame seeds

On a slice of bread add a large lettuce cup. Fill with ½ cup low fat cottage cheese, sprinkle over 1 teaspoon of toasted sesame seeds, some chopped shallots and thin slices of radish.

tomato and sprouts

On a slice of bread pile on mixed sprouts (alfalfa and mung), thinly sliced tomatoes and onion rings. Season with 2 teaspoons finely chopped parsley and basil.

gourmet roll

Choose a well rounded medium roll. You might like to make your own or select a suitable wholemeal roll or rye roll.

Cut 2cm slits in the roll from top to bottom without cutting right through. Ease roll open slightly. Fill the gaps with fillings of your choice. This is an excellent idea for a picnic hamper.

Some Ideas:

- Lettuce pieces, spring onions, alfalfa sprouts, slices of red apple.

- Slices of cucumber, tomato and onion rings, tomato chutney.

- Slices of radish, grated carrot, lettuce pieces and thinly sliced mushrooms, low fat cottage cheese and lemon juice (beat together).

- Thin slices of pineapple, thin slices of low fat cheese, thin slices of fresh zucchini, low fat ricotta cheese and orange juice (beat together).

- Low fat cottage cheese, mashed banana, sultanas, dash of cinnamon.

- Lettuce pieces, slices of fresh pear and thin slices of celery, date and apple chutney.

- Shredded cabbage, strips of red pepper, onion rings, and carrot strips. Sprinkle finely chopped parsley and fresh tarragon over roll.

special occasion sandwiches
circle sandwiches

Choose a suitable wholemeal salt free/sugar free and fat free bread. Using a champagne glass (or similar cutter) cut out circles of bread. Keep crusts for breadcrumbs at a later stage.

Spread one side of the circle with a suitable spread. Top with your favorite filling combinations and place on lid.

Serve whole or cut in half.

Some Ideas:
- Spread with tomato chutney, add slices of tomato, shredded lettuce, onion rings and thin slices of cucumber.

- Spread with date and apple chutney, add bean shoots, carrot strips (use peeler to peel long fine strips of carrot) and grated raw beetroot.

- Spread with cottage cheese. Add chopped shallots, finely chopped celery, freshly cooked asparagus spears mashed.

- Spread with cottage cheese, chopped cress, thinly sliced radishes, slices of tomato, alfalfa sprouts. Spread the top layer with a spread of your choice, for example, tomato chutney, date and apple chutney.

- Spread with cottage cheese, mashed bananas, sultanas and a dash of cinnamon.

- Spread with date and apple chutney, mashed banana and thin slices of apple.

the dagwood

Use thickly sliced wholemeal bread. Top it with any fruits or vegetables, or a combination of both; any left-over vegetable dishes, for example, a spaghetti tomato vegetable sauce; any left-over cold chicken or fish roughly chopped. Keep the layers going until the appetite feels its just reward.

Keep a fresh wholemeal loaf of bread handy with a sharp bread knife, and a container of ready made fillings and they can be made as needed. A spread is not necessarily needed but you might like to choose from those suggested.

Filling Suggestions:
Vegetables

lettuce cups
shredded lettuce
endive leaves
sorrel leaves
cress
shredded green or red cabbage
celery (sliced thinly)
fennel (finely chopped)
asparagus (lightly steamed, cold)
cucumber (sliced)
mashed cold cooked pumpkin
zucchini (grated, raw)
beetroot (grated, raw) or lightly cooked and sliced onions
carrot (strips or grated raw)
potato (peeled lightly cooked, cold)
corn (cooked and kernels removed from cob, cold)
green beans (finely chopped)
tomatoes (sliced)
capsicum (sliced thinly in strips or circles)
button mushrooms (thinly sliced)
alfalfa sprouts
bean shoots

Fruits:
banana (sliced or mashed)
apple (grated or thinly sliced or lightly cooked, cold)
pears (thinly sliced or lightly cooked, cold)
pineapple (very thinly sliced)
berries

Others:
steamed chicken (chop roughly)
steamed fish (left-overs)
egg white (roughly chopped)
rice (cooked, cold)
wholemeal pasta (cooked, cold)
dried apples (chopped)
dried apricots (chopped)
sultanas

spreads

With advertising as it is today, we seem to be able to justify a 'dob' of butter on just about everything. I've always found it hard to believe that the so called 'dob' of butter was responsible for bringing out the true flavour of whatever it was you added to it.

Nathan Pritikin quite clearly points out the harmful qualities of polyunsaturates and butter in relationship to some cancers and heart disease in The Pritikin Promise. 28 Days to a Longer Healthier Life. Bantam books, p. 40, p. 63, pp. 380–83, pp. 405–6.

If we give the true flavour of wholegrain breads a chance, we soon discover that 'real bread' tastes great, without the need to add anything. However, if you still need to spread a dash of interest and low fat flavour, here are a few suggestions.

basic spread

½ cup non-fat cottage cheese
2 tbsps skim milk (just enough to
    bind and make smooth)

A good squeeze of lemon juice.

Beat together until smooth. Spread.

green pepper spread

½ cup non-fat cottage cheese
2 tbsps skim milk
2–3 tbsps finely chopped green
    capsicum

A good grinding of fresh black
    peppercorns

Beat together until smooth. Spread.

51

herb spread

½ cup non-fat cottage cheese
2 tbsps skim milk

2–3 tbsps finely chopped fresh
  herbs (parsley, chives, basil
  garlic chives)

Beat together until smooth. Spread.

mustard spread

½ cup non-fat cottage cheese
1–2 tbsps dijon mustard (just
  enough to satisfy the taste buds)

Beat together until smooth. Spread.

tomato chutney spread

makes 4 litres (approximately)

4 large onions, peeled and diced
3kg ripe tomatoes, peeled and
  chopped
6 large granny smith apples
3 cloves garlic crushed
4 cups cider vinegar
250g sultanas

1 cup raisins
1 teaspoon allspice
1 teaspoon mace
1 teaspoon cloves
1 teaspoon chilli powder
1 cup unsweetened orange juice

Combine all ingredients in a large saucepan. Bring to the boil. Boil for 1 hour uncovered, stirring frequently. Remove from heat. Pour into warm bottles.

Process in usual method.

Suggested uses:
Pizza base. Sandwich spread. Salad dressing.
Note: Once opened, keep refrigerated.

sweet spreads

These spreads are basically fresh fruits set with a gel-like substance called agar-agar. It is a natural seaweed gelatin. It comes in a powdered form of which approximately 1 teaspoon will set 300 ml (1¼ cups) liquid, or in a bar approximately 26 cm long. One bar of agar-agar will set approximately three cups of liquid.

These are only approximate, because different gelling consistencies are desired by different people.

I usually make up a small quantity of spread as needed with whatever fruit is in season. However, if you are going to invest in the Preserving Unit we talked about in the Home Preserves Section, you could make up large batches of spreads and follow the instructions to preserve in the usual way. (Now you can store your spreads on the shelf – otherwise spreads should be refrigerated.)

blueberry jam spread

makes approximately 3 cups

When blueberries are in season, this will undoubtedly become one of your favourite spreads!

1½cups unsweetened natural pear juice	450g blueberries
	1 tbsp lemon juice
⅓ cup apple juice concentrate	2 teaspoons agar-agar

Combine pear juice, lemon juice, apple juice concentrate and agar-agar in a saucepan. Slowly bring to the boil, stirring to dissolve the agar-agar. Boil for 5 minutes. Add blueberries and boil for another 10 minutes. Pour into sterilized jars. Keep refrigerated.

cherry spread

makes approximately 3 cups

1 cup unsweetened orange juice	½ bar agar-agar (cut into small pieces)
1 cup apple juice concentrate	
1 tbsp lemon juice	500g stoned cherries
¼ teaspoon lemon rind	

Place the first five ingredients in a saucepan. Slowly bring to the boil. Simmer for fifteen minutes stirring occasionally. Add cherries. Slowly bring to the boil again. Simmer for five minutes. Pour into sterilized jars. Cool. Refrigerate.

clear marmalade

makes approximately 1¼ cups

1½ cups clear apple and pear juice
2 teaspoons apple juice concentrate

1 teaspoon agar-agar powder
1 teaspoon finely grated lemon zest

Place all ingredients in a saucepan. Slowly bring to the boil, stirring to dissolve agar-agar. As mixture comes to the boil, turn down to simmer. Simmer for five minutes. Remove from heat and pour into a sterilized jar. As mixture begins to set, stir with a spoon to keep the lemon rind evenly distributed through the spread. Cool. Refrigerate.

fresh apricot spread

makes approximately 3 cups

1 cup unsweetened apple and pear
    juice
1 cup unsweetened orange juice
½ cup apple juice concentrate

2 teaspoons agar-agar powder
½–1 tbsp lemon juice
400g roughly chopped fresh
    apricots (stones removed)

Place the first five ingredients in a saucepan and slowly bring to the boil. Simmer for five minutes. Add apricots and simmer for 15–20 minutes. Remove from heat. Pour into sterilized jars. Cool. Refrigerate.

raspberry spread

makes approximately 3½ cups

1¼ cups clear apple and pear juice
2 teaspoons agar-agar

¼ cup apple juice concentrate
450g raspberries

Place apple and pear juice, agar-agar and apple juice concentrates in a saucepan. Slowly bring to the boil. Simmer for five minutes. Add raspberries. Slowly bring to the boil again. Simmer for five minutes. Remove from heat. Pour into sterilized jars. Cool. Refrigerate.

strawberry spread

makes approximately 6 cups

2 cups unsweetened apple and pear or
2 cups unsweetened orange juice
4 teaspoons agar-gar

¾ cup apple juice concentrate
1 kg strawberries

Place the first three ingredients in a saucepan and slowly bring to the boil. Simmer for five minutes. Add strawberries. Bring to the boil again., Simmer for 20–25 minutes. Remove from heat. Pour into sterilized jars. Cool. Refrigerate.

salads for one

A salad should be a meal of colour, shape, texture and delectable flavours enhanced occasionally with herbs, a simple dressing, and a dash of presentation.

A salad can be a meal for many, served just on its own, or served with an accompaniment like home-made vegetable sausages.

This selection is reserved for Salads for One. They can be a meal, or an entrée or you might like to increase the quantity of ingredients to cater for larger numbers.

Most developed countries are truly fortunate to have such a wide variety of fresh fruits and vegetables nearly all year round. Make the salad a big part of your daily menu.

asparagus and orange salad

2 lettuce leaves (preferably cos lettuce)
4 slices of orange rounds, peel removed
6–8 pieces of lightly cooked asparagus
¼ red capsicum, cut into thin strips
2 tbsps curry dressing (see Dressings section)
4 radishes, cut into julienne strips
4 sprigs of parsley

Place the lettuce leaves on a dinner plate. Overlap orange slices on top of lettuce. Add asparagus and capsicum. Pour over dressing. Sprinkle radish over dressing and garnish with parsley sprigs. (The parsley is not just a garnish, but an important part of the meal.)

cantaloup with prawns

3 mignonette lettuce leaves
½ cantaloup (well chilled)
90g small prawns, shelled and
    deveined
¼ cup grated cucumber flesh
¼ cup grated apple

2 tbsps lemon juice
2 teaspoons fresh dill finely
    chopped
½ cup red capsicum strips
2 tbsps mayonnaise and 2 teaspoons
    tomato paste, combined well.

Remove seeds from cantaloup and peel. Cut out a U-shape on one side of the cantaloup, (so the filling can fall out onto the lettuce). Combine prawns, cucumber, apple, lemon juice and dill. Refrigerate for 1 hour.

Add capsicum and toss through. Place the lettuce on a dinner plate. Sit cantaloup on lettuce and spoon filling into its centre. Let some filling fall out on the lettuce. Spoon over dressing. Serve.

chicken hawaii salad

90g cooked chicken, broken up
¼ cup cooked corn kernels
¼ cup crushed unsweetened
    pineapple
¼ cup green capsicum strips
4 cauliflower flowerettes (If you
    don't like them raw, drop them

into boiling water for 2 minutes.
    Drain. Plunge into chilled water.
    Drain.)
½–1 cup mung bean sprouts
4 cherry tomatoes cut in half
¼ cup spicy tomato dressing (see
    Dressings section)

Combine all ingredients and toss through dressing. Refrigerate for at least 1 hour. Spoon into a bowl. Serve.

chilli beans salad

4 slices of tomato
4 slices of orange, peeled
1 cup cooked red kidney beans
small clove garlic crushed
¼ teaspoon chilli powder

¼ cup red capsicum strips
2 tbsps chopped spring onions
¼ cup green capsicum chopped
2 tbsps unsweetened orange juice
1 tbsp white wine vinegar

Arrange tomato and orange slices on a dinner plate. Combine all the ingredients and mix well. Spoon bean mixture over tomato and orange slices.

cucumber boats salad

¼ lettuce
½ cucumber, peeled, seeds
  removed
8 lightly cooked asparagus spears
  (for asparagus cooking
  instructions, see *Taste of Life*)

½ cup alfalfa sprouts
6 snow peas to garnish
2 teaspoons finely grated lemon
  rind
¼ cup herb vinaigrette

Place the ¼ of lettuce alongside the cucumber boat on a dinner plate. Arrange asparagus spears in the cucumber boat. Garnish the cucumber boat with the sprouts and snow peas to one end of the lettuce and cucumber. Sprinkle lemon rind over asparagus. Pour herb vinaigrette over all the ingredients.

cucumber red-slaw salad

All ingredients should be well chilled.

1 small cucumber
1 cup finely shredded red cabbage
1 jonathan apple, core and cut into
  julienne strips
2 tbsps finely chopped odourless
  onion

¼ teaspoon dried caraway seed
2 tbsp mayonnaise (see Dressings
  section)
1 tbsp roasted pine nuts (to roast
  pine nuts, place on a non-stick
  baking pan over heat. Move
  them continuously until lightly
  browned.)

Peel cucumber and cut in half lengthwise. Scoop out seeds, leaving a hollow space. Combine cabbage, apple, onion, caraway seed and mayonnaise. Toss well. Place both cucumber halves on a dinner plate. Spoon cabbage and apple mixture into the hollows and let overflow onto dinner plate.

curried pineapple and potato salad

½ pineapple (green part also)
1 large potato
½ cup chopped celery
½ cup green grapes

¼ cup cooked green peas
¼ cup curry dressing (see
  Dressings section)

Carefully remove pineapple flesh and chop up. Thoroughly wash the potato and steam in its jacket until tender. Cut into cubes. Plunge into cold water. Drain. Combine all ingredients and toss. Spoon back into pineapple shell. Serve.

egg and cucumber salad

2 hard boiled eggs
½ cup chopped cucumber cubes –
   remove seeds and peel
½ cup chopped celery cubes
½ cup chopped apple cubes
½ cup chopped cooked, peeled
   potato cubes

2 tbsps mayonnaise (see Dressings
   section)
slices of cucumber
endive

Shell the eggs. Carefully cut in half and remove yolk. Chop up egg whites to approximately the same size as other ingredients. Combine all ingredients except cucumber slices and endive. Toss in the mayonnaise to coat well. Arrange curly endive on a dinner plate, top with cucumber slices and spoon over egg and cucumber mixture. Serve.

lobster salad

1 large lettuce leaf (soak in chilled
   water so it will curl up to make
   crisp cup shape)
4 slices cooked beetroot
90g lobster
6 orange segments

3 slices honeydew melon
2 slices of kiwi fruit to garnish
2 teaspoons finely grated orange rind
¼ cup orange curried sauce (see
   Dressings section)

Place lettuce cup on a dinner plate. Add beetroot slices, lobster to one side, orange segments on the other. Place melon slices alongside the lettuce cup and kiwi fruit at one end of the melon slices. Sprinkle over with the orange rind and spoon over the dressing. Serve.

macaroni mint and corn salad

3 sorrel leaves, washed and dried
1 cup cooked wholemeal macaroni
1 granny smith apple, cored and cut
   into thin slices
1 small zucchini, cut into julienne

strips – steam for 2 minutes in
   boiling water and plunge in cold
   water, drain
4 spring onions chopped
1 cup cooked corn kernels

Dressing:

¼ cup vinaigrette

2 tbsps unsweetened orange juice

1 tbsp finely chopped mint

Combine ingredients.

Arrange sorrel leaves on a dinner plate. Combine macaroni, apple, zucchini, onions and corn. Pour over dressing and toss. Spoon onto sorrel leaves. Serve.

melon and raisin salad

3 lettuce leaves (cos lettuce, known also as romaine lettuce, will create interest in this salad)

3 wedge slices of honeydew melon

3 slices watermelon (seeds removed)

1 kiwi fruit

2 slices of odourless onion (break up the rings)

3 tbsps raisins

¼ cup vinaigrette of your choice or spice fruit dressing (2 tbsps only, see Dressings section)

All ingredients except onion and raisins should be chilled. Soak the raisins in the vinaigrette for at least 1 hour. Drain.

Arrange ingredients on a dinner plate in order listed. Scatter over the raisins and pour over the dressing.

orange and nectarine salad

1 large cabbage leaf

2 baby carrots cut into rounds

1 orange peeled and segmented

2 nectarines, remove stone and cut into thin slices

2 tbsps non-fat or low fat cottage cheese

1 tbsp currants

shake of nutmeg

Drop cabbage leaf and carrot into boiling water for 2 minutes. Drain. Plunge in chilled water. Drain.

Place the cabbage leaf on a dinner plate. Arrange the orange, nectarine and carrot rounds on the cabbage leaf. Mix the cottage cheese and currants together. Spoon onto cabbage leaf at one end. Add a shake of nutmeg to taste. Serve.

pear bean salad

cress (desired quantity)
1 pear, peeled and cooked until just
 tender
½ cup cooked red kidney beans
½ cup cooked baby lima beans
¼ cup unsweetened pineapple
 pieces
¼ cup green capsicum strips
2 tbsps odourless onion diced
¼ cup cucumber cubes (peel and
 remove cucumber seeds)
¼ cup grated zucchini
2 tbsps mayonnaise (see Dressings
 section)

Spread the cress on a dinner plate to make a circle. Cut pear in half
and remove core. Position the pear halves side by side in the circle.
Combine all other ingredients and toss well. Spoon over pear and on
to the plate inside the cress circle.

salmon coleslaw salad

½ cup finely shredded savoy
 cabbage (crinkly leaves)
½ cup finely shredded red cabbage
2 tbsps chopped spring onions
¼ cup finely sliced celery
¼ cup crushed unsweetened
 pineapple
90g flaked salmon (water packed or
 lightly steamed fresh salmon)
2 tbsps mustard dressing (see
 Dressings section)

Combine all ingredients and toss well. Refrigerate for at least 2 hours
before serving. Spoon into a bowl. Serve.

savoury apple salad

1 large granny smith apple
¼ cup lemon juice
1 cup chilled water
2 tbsps non-fat cottage cheese
small clove of garlic crushed
pinch of dried tarragon or dill
endive leaves
1 grapefruit, peeled and segmented
1 cup cucumber moons. (Peel
 cucumber, cut in half lengthwise
 and scoop out the seeds. Place
 on a chopping board, round side
 up. Using a sharp knife slice
 along the cucumber about ½cm
 apart.)

Peel the top half of the apple, and remove core. Combine lemon juice
and water. Soak apple for 10 minutes. Drain.

Combine cottage cheese, garlic and tarragon. Mix well. Spoon into
the centre of the apple and push down. Wrap apple in foil and
refrigerate for 1 hour.

Arrange the endive leaves on a dinner plate. Place apple to one side. Scatter over the grapefruit and cucumber. You might like to pour over a little vinaigrette, but it is not a necessity, as the fruit and cucumber should be moist enough.

spinach and sprouts salad

2 spinach leaves
2 lettuce leaves
4 slices tomato
4 slices cucumber (peel removed)
½ cup bean shoots

½ cup alfalfa sprouts
½ cup lentil sprouts
¼ cup spicy tomato dressing (see Dressings section)

Wash and shake dry the spinach and lettuce leaves. Shred finely together. Arrange the shredded spinach and lettuce (combine together) at either end of a dinner plate. Arrange 2 slices of tomato and 2 slices of cucumber at each end, on top of spinach and lettuce. Combine bean shoots and sprouts and toss in dressing. Serve these in the centre of the dish.

spinach with water chestnuts

1 cup shredded spinach
1 cup shredded lettuce
90g cooked chicken, roughly chopped
¼ cup sliced water chestnuts

2 tbsps chopped chives
½ cup wholemeal bread cubes
1 tbsp garlic powder
2 tbsps vinaigrette of your choice

Toss spinach and lettuce to combine. Add chicken and water chestnuts. Sprinkle over chopped chives. Toss bread cubes with garlic powder. Shake off excess garlic powder. Place on a non-stick baking tray. Place in a hot oven for 10 minutes or until well browned. Add vinaigrette to salad and lightly toss. Add garlic bread cubes. Serve.

tuna salad

3 lettuce leaves
1 medium tomato
½ cup cooked peas
2 teaspoons finely chopped mint
3 baby carrots, washed (peeled if necessary)

80g tuna (water packed)
½ lemon
2 tbsps finely chopped spring onions
4 green capsicum rings

Slice the top off the tomato. Scoop out the seeds and flesh. Discard. Combine peas and mint and spoon into tomato case. Refrigerate. Drop carrots into boiling water. Cook for 3 minutes. Drain. Plunge into cold water. Drain. Squeeze lemon over tuna and add onion. Place lettuce leaves on a dinner plate and position the tomato on the lettuce leaves to one side. Place carrots side by side in front and tuna at their sides on the green capsicum rings.

turkey and soyaroni salad

1 cup cooked soyaroni noodles
90g cooked turkey, broken up
4 cauliflower flowerettes
4 broccoli flowerettes

2 baby carrots, cut into thin rounds
4 medium mushrooms, thoroughly
    washed and sliced

Dressing:
½ cup unsweetened orange juice
1 clove garlic crushed
1 teaspoon fresh ginger juice (use a
    garlic press)

Combine dressing ingredients in a small saucepan. Add cauliflower, broccoli, carrot and mushrooms. Slowly bring to the boil. Simmer for 2 minutes stirring continuously. Remove from heat. Drain vegetables. Set aside liquid. Place vegetables into a chilled container. Leave to cool. Refrigerate. When liquid has cooled refrigerate also.

To serve, combine all ingredients and remaining liquid dressing. Serve on a glass plate (dinner plate size.)

vegetarian salad

Although a lot of salads in this section would suit a vegetarian palate, I like the simplicity of this salad, and its presentation. Use a round platter and arrange as follows.

1 ½ cup grated carrot
2 6 green beans (Top and tail and cook in boiling water for 3 minutes. Drain. Plunge into cold water. Drain.)
3 30g finely grated low fat cheese
4 6 slices of tomato
5 ½ cup sprouts (alfalfa, mung or lentil)
6 ½ cup cucumber strips (peel, remove seeds and cut into 4cm lengths)

7 ½ cup raw beetroot, grated
8 1 small jonathan apple, cored and cut into thin wedges.
9 parsley rice mould (Cook ¼ cup brown rice in boiling water. Drain. Fold through 2 tablespoons of finely chopped spring onions and 2 tablespoons of finely chopped parsley. Press into a small mould and cool. Refrigerate for at least 2 hours before removing from mould.)

Serve this salad with a selection of dressings.

dressings

A dressing should complement the salad – not overpower it.

creamy cottage cheese dressing

makes approximately 1 cup

200g low fat cottage cheese
1 tbsp apple juice concentrate
1 tbsp tarragon vinegar

¼ cup of unsweetened apple or
   pineapple juice

Combine all ingredients in a blender and process until thick and creamy. Refrigerate.

curry dressing

makes approximately ½ cup

½ cup non-fat yoghurt
1 teaspoon curry powder

1 teaspoon tomato paste (salt free)
1 tbsp unsweetened orange juice

Mix all ingredients thoroughly and keep refrigerated.

garlic vinaigrette

makes approximately 1¼ cups

¾ cup apple juice
½ cup white wine vinegar
2 tbsps lemon juice

2 teaspoons grated lemon rind
4 small cloves garlic peeled and cut
   in half

Combine all ingredients in a screw top jar and keep in refrigerator. Shake every now and then. Remove garlic prior to serving, or remove and crush then return to vinaigrette.

herb vinaigrette

makes approximately 1¼ cups

¾ cup unsweetened orange juice
½ cup white wine vinegar
2 tbsps finely chopped fresh
  oregano

2 tbsps finely chopped fresh chives
2 tbsps finely chopped fresh parsley

Combine all ingredients and mix well. Store in refrigerator.

mayonnaise

makes 2 cups

¾ cup low fat evaporated milk
¼ cup apple juice concentrate

2 teaspoons dijon mustard
½ cup wine vinegar

Place ingredients in a screw top jar and shake well. Store in refrigerator. Shake well before each use.

mustard dressing

makes approximately 1 cup

1 cup non-fat yoghurt
1 teaspoon dry mustard

1 tbsp dijon mustard
1 tbsp tarragon vinegar

Mix the dry mustard with a small amount of the yoghurt to blend in thoroughly. Add this to all other ingredients. Mix well. Store in refrigerator.

orange curried sauce

makes 1 cup.

1 cup unsweetened orange juice

1–2 teaspoons curry powder
2 teaspoons arrowroot

Mix the arrowroot and curry powder with a small amount of the orange juice to make a paste. Stir through remaining orange juice. Place in a small saucepan. Slowly bring to the boil until sauce thickens. Cool. Refrigerate.

Use as required. Excellent over chicken, turkey, cantaloup, cucumbers and pineapple.

spice fruit dressing

makes approximately 1/2 cup

½ cup non-fat yoghurt
¼ teaspoon allspice

¼ teaspoon nutmeg
1 tbsp unsweetened orange juice

Combine all ingredients and mix well. Store in refrigerator.

spicy tomato dressing

makes approximately 2¼ cups

1 cup tomato juice (salt free)
1 cup unsweetened orange juice
rind of 1 orange finely grated
¼ cup white wine vinegar
2 small cloves garlic

½ teaspoon dried oregano
½ teaspoon dried basil
dash of cayenne pepper
3 teaspoons arrowroot
1 tbsp water

Combine the first 8 ingredients in a saucepan and slowly bring to the boil. Mix arrowroot with the water and stir through to thicken. Simmer for 2 minutes. Leave to cool. Store in the refrigerator. Remove garlic before using.

vinaigrette dressing

makes approximately 1¼ cups

¾ cup apple juice
½ cup white wine vinegar
1 teaspoon dry mustard
sprig of fresh rosemary
   (approximately 6cm)

6 black peppercorns (remove before
   using dressing)
2 teaspoons orange rind
1 tbsp lemon juice
1 tbsp apple juice concentrate

Combine all ingredients in a screw top jar and keep in refrigerator. Shake every now and then.

our favourites

This section is reserved for our favourite main meals, suitable for lunches, dinners or special nights with friends.

artichoke and mushroom salad

serves 3–4

250g button mushrooms, halved
440g artichoke hearts, cooked
1 cup chopped celery
1 cup cherry tomatoes
1 green capsicum, roughly chopped
⅔ cup wine vinegar

⅔ cup unsweetened orange juice
2 cloves garlic, crushed
1 teaspoon dried basil
1 teaspoon oregano
1 teaspoon finely grated orange rind

To cook the artichokes, remove the outer leaves and break off the stalk. Cut across the top leaf part of the artichoke. Discard the outer dark green leaves. Drop each artichoke in water to which the juice of 1 lemon has been added. Drop them into boiling water. Cook for 30 to 45 minutes depending on the size of the artichoke. They should be tender. Scoop out the fuzzy centre and leave to cool.

Wash and drain mushrooms. Combine all the vegetables and artichokes.

Combine the last 6 ingredients in a saucepan. Simmer for 10 minutes. Pour over vegetables and stir to coat. Cover. When cool enough, refrigerate for at least 3 hours. Drain vegetables and serve on a bed of finely shredded cabbage.

cabbage and potatoes

serves 1

2 small tomatoes, peeled and
    seeded
¼ cup mustard dressing
¼ teaspoon caraway seed

¼ wedge of a cabbage, lightly
    steamed
3 medium potatoes, steamed

Chop tomatoes and place in a small saucepan. Cook for 2 minutes.
Add mustard dressing and caraway seeds. Stir to heat through. Pour
over potatoes on a dinner plate. Position cooked cabbage beside
potatoes and serve.

carrot mousse with white parsley sauce

serves 4

500g carrots (preferably baby
    carrots)
2 teaspoons fresh ginger juice
¼ cup wholemeal plain flour

1 cup low fat evaporated milk
¼ teaspoon nutmeg
4 egg whites

White Parsley Sauce:

1½ cups skim milk
2 tbsps cornflour
2 tbsps finely chopped parsley

black ground pepper to taste
    (optional)

To make mousse:
Cook carrots until just tender. Place in a food processor and process
until smooth with ginger. Place flour in a small saucepan on low heat
for a few seconds. Pour in milk stirring briskly until thickened. Add
nutmeg. Pour over carrots in the blender and process until all ingredients are combined. Add egg whites and process for 15 seconds.
Pour into lightly greased individual moulds. Cover with foil. Place in
a water bath. Bake at 180°C for 40 minutes. Remove from oven and
let stand for 5 minutes before turning out. Serve with white parsley
sauce, steamed broccoli and cherry tomatoes.

To make sauce:
Combine a little milk with the cornflour and make a paste. Heat
remaining milk until boiling. Stir in cornflour. Cook until sauce
thickens, and add parsley.

chicken and carrot roll

serves 4–6

Filling:
2 chicken fillets
2 large grated carrots
1 medium onion
2 granny smith apples
¾ cup green capsicum

¾ cup green beans
½ cup celery
3 heaped teaspoons fresh herbs
    (lemon balm, parsley)
3 sheets wholemeal filo pastry

Topping:
½ cup finely chopped celery leaves
½ cup finely chopped parsley

1 egg white

To make filling:
Chop chicken into small pieces. Combine with remaining filling ingredients and mix well. Lie the pastry flat on a non-stick baking tray. Spoon filling along one end of the pastry leaving enough room at each end to fold over. Roll over until all pastry is used.

To make topping:
Combine celery leaves and parsley. Wipe the top of the roll with egg white. Sprinkle over the celery leaves and parsley. Cook at 180°C for 50 minutes.

    Serve with a salad.

chicken and ginger zucchini balls

serves 4–6
makes 16–20

360g chicken meat (all visible fat and
    skin removed)
2 granny smith apples, peeled and
    grated
1 medium onion, peeled and chopped

2 medium zucchini, grated
1 teaspoon finely grated fresh ginger
1 teaspoon finely grated lemon rind
1 cup wholemeal breadcrumbs

Combine chicken, apples and onions in a food processor. Process until smooth. Remove from food processor bowl and add zucchini, ginger and lemon. Mix well. Take a dessertspoonful of mixture and roll into a ball. Roll in breadcrumbs.

    Place on a lightly greased oven tray and cook at 200°C for 30–40 minutes or until lightly browned.

    Serve with a selection of salads.

cucumber fish with marinated mushrooms

serves 6

6 (90g) fish fillets
¼ cup lemon juice
1 cup chopped leek
1 cucumber peeled

½ cup vegetable/chicken stock
4 tomatoes, or equivalent in bottle
  tomatoes
1 small green pepper cut into strips

Sauce:

2 tbsps water
2 tbsps cornflour

2 tbsps parsley, finely chopped

Marinated Mushrooms:

3 cups finely sliced mushrooms
1 cup unsweetened orange juice

2 tbsps tarragon vinegar
¼ cup fresh chopped herbs
  (parsley, chives, basil)

Pour lemon juice over fish in a bowl and leave for 10 minutes. Cut cucumber into 4 pieces. Using a sharp pointed knife carefully remove seeds, leaving a hollow. Slice into rounds. Add chopped leek and cucumber rounds to a small non-stick frypan. Pour over stock. Cover and simmer for 10 minutes. Add tomato and pepper, cover and cook for a further 5 minutes over a low heat. Remove lid.

Place fish fillets on top of vegetables. Add any remaining lemon juice to the sauce ingredients and make a paste. Cover the fish and cook for 3 minutes.

Place the fish and vegetables on the serving plates. Add sauce ingredients to remaining juice in the pan and slowly bring to the boil stirring continuously. When sauce thickens, remove from heat and spoon over the fish. Serve with lightly steamed broccoli and marinated mushrooms.

To make marinated mushrooms:

Combine marinade ingredients and marinate in refrigerator for at least 2 hours.

filled baked butternut pumpkin

serves 2

1 medium butternut pumpkin
1 clove garlic crushed
2 tbsps onion finely chopped
2 tbsps finely chopped red
    capsicum
180g minced beef (all visible fat
    removed)
½–1 teaspoon ground cumin

1 cup grated carrot
2 large chopped tomatoes, peeled
    and seeded
1 cup cooked brown rice
1 cup wholemeal breadcrumbs
2 tbsps finely grated low fat grating
    cheese

Cut pumpkin in half lengthways. Scoop out seeds and good part of the pumpkin flesh to leave a deep cavity. Crush garlic, add onion, capsicum and meat in a small saucepan. Add a small amount of water. Cook on low heat for 20 minutes or until meat is tender. Turn frequently. Add spices, grated carrot and tomatoes. Cover and cook over gentle heat for a further 5 minutes. Add more liquid if necessary (however, mixture should be fairly dry). Remove from heat and fold in rice.

Spoon equal quantities of mixture into the two pumpkin halves. Top with breadcrumbs and sprinkle over equal quantities of the cheese. Place in an oven bag or a baking tray, and cover with foil. Cook at 200°C for 40 to 45 minutes or until top is well browned.

fish and spinach rolls

serves 6

12 large spinach/silver beet (white
    part removed) leaves
400g suitable fish fillets
juice of ½ lemon
2 medium carrots, grated
¼ cup finely chopped leeks or ½
    cup chopped spring onions

½ cup thinly sliced water chestnuts
    (packed in water)
½ teaspoon fresh ginger juice and
    pulp
2 teaspoons finely grated lemon rind
½ cup cooked brown rice or grated
    apple

Sauce:

½ cup tomato juice (salt free)
¾ cup unsweetened orange juice
¼ cup chopped parsley
1 tbsp cornflour

Wash spinach/silver beet leaves thoroughly under hot water. Place fillets in a food processor. Using the chopping blade, mince fish fillets. Add all other ingredients and mix well. Lay two leaves on top of each other to make a large area to roll around the filling. Repeat until all leaves are used. Divide filling equally between leaves. Roll up and place side by side in a large steamer. With lid on, cook for 35 minutes.

Sauce:
Combine all ingredients and mix thoroughly. Simmer until sauce thickens. Pour over fish and spinach rolls and serve with a baked potato and a tossed salad.

fish mornay

serves 6

Filling:
2 tbsps wholemeal plain flour
¾ cup skim milk
¼ cup dry white wine
½ cup low fat evaporated skim milk
50g finely grated low fat grating
    cheese

500g cooked fish fillets
250g grated apple
1 cup finely chopped spring onions

Base:
2 cups cooked wholemeal brown
    rice
½ cup finely chopped spinach

½ cup finely chopped leek
2 tbsps water

Topping:
1 cup wholemeal breadcrumbs

½ cup finely chopped celery leaves

To make base:
Combine base ingredients and spoon into a lightly greased oven baking dish. Pour fish mixture over rice.

To make filling:
Place flour in a saucepan. Stir over low heat for a few seconds. Pour in milk and stir briskly, until quite smooth. Add wine and gently bring to the boil until sauce thickens. Add evaporated skim milk and cheese. Stir until cheese melts. Combine fish (broken into small pieces), grated apple and spring onions. Add to sauce.

To make topping:
Sprinkle combined breadcrumbs and celery over filling. Bake at 180°C uncovered for 30 minutes.

fish parcels

serves 4

4 (90g) flounder fillets
4 tbsps finely grated low fat grating
   cheese
8 medium mushrooms, thinly sliced
¼ cup non-fat yoghurt
1 tbsp finely chopped chives
2 tbsps finely chopped red
   capsicum

cayenne pepper to taste.
16 julienne strips of carrot
1 tbsp non-fat yoghurt (extra)
1 egg white
¼ cup wholemeal breadcrumbs,
   toasted

Spread fillets out flat to make a rectangle (pound slightly, if necessary). Combine cheese, mushrooms, yoghurt, chives, capsicum and cayenne. Mix well. Spread evenly over each fillet. Place 4 carrot strips on each fillet and carefully roll up. Place seam side down in a lightly greased shallow baking dish. Combine yoghurt and egg white. Using a pastry brush, wipe the tops of fish and sprinkle over the breadcrumbs.

Bake at 180°C for 20 minutes. Serve with a salad.

summer garden salad with tofu

In a large salad bowl, combine the following ingredients in the following order.

broken lettuce leaves
finely shredded cabbage
salad onion rings
julienne strips of carrot
julienne strips of parsnip (small,
   sweet ones)
thin rounds of zucchini (small,
   sweet ones)
green beans cut into 2 cm lengths

tomato wedges
tofu cut into 2 cm squares (allow
   approximately 70g per person)
¾ cup finely chopped fresh mixed
   herbs, (parsley, chives, mint,
   basil, oregano, thyme etc)
¼ cup freshly squeezed lemon
   juice
¼ cup wine vinegar (or tarragon)

Sprinkle herbs over salad. Combine lemon juice and vinegar and pour over salad.

hot prawn and orange salad

serves 4 as an entrée

12 prawns
1½ cups wholemeal pasta (I prefer
    wholemeal noodle shells). You
    may also like to use wholemeal
    spaghetti
½ cup unsweetened orange juice
½ cup vegetable stock/water
2 tbsps fresh oregano
1–2 cloves garlic, crushed (optional)

24 snow peas
24 carrot strips
1 cup finely shredded red cabbage
1 tbsp pine nuts
segments of 2 oranges
juice of 1 lemon
¼ cup chopped chives

Shell prawns, leaving on tails. Make a slit down the back of each prawn and remove the black vein. Rinse in cold water. Drop the pasta in boiling water and simmer until cooked (should be slightly firm).

While pasta is cooking add orange juice, vegetable stock/water, oregano and garlic to a wok/pan and bring to the boil, turn heat down to a gentle simmer, add snow peas, carrot, red cabbage and pine nuts. Move around quickly with a wooden spatula for 1 minute. Add prawns and keep moving for further 2 minutes coating prawns and vegetables in the liquid. Add orange segments on top. Turn heat up so nearly all liquid is absorbed and oranges are heated through. Remove from heat.

Drain pasta. Add lemon juice and chives and toss well. Place equal quantity of pasta on each serving plate and spoon over hot prawns and orange salad.

To serve as a main meal, increase the amount of wholemeal pasta used.

lemon, herbed spinach spaghetti

serves 4–6

500g wholemeal spaghetti
1 cup spinach, finely chopped
1 cup mixed finely chopped herbs
    (parsley, chives, oregano, basil)

1 cup very finely sliced celery
¼ cup lemon juice
¼ cup currants
1 cup alfalfa sprouts or mung

Cook spaghetti in boiling water. While spaghetti is cooking, place spinach in a small amount of water. Bring to the boil and simmer for 3 minutes. Drain. Drain spaghetti when cooked. Fold in all ingredients and serve immediately.

mushroom pie

serves 6–8

Base:

2 cups wholemeal breadcrumbs
½ cup finely chopped shallots

1 egg white
1 tbsp toasted sesame seeds

Filling:

3 medium grated zucchini
2 medium sliced tomatoes
1 teaspoon basil (dried)
1 teaspoon oregano (dried)
200g mushrooms, thinly sliced
4 egg whites

½ cup low fat evaporated milk
1 cup parsley (finely chopped)
¼ cup non-fat yoghurt
¼ cup low fat grating cheese
1 cup wholemeal breadcrumbs

To make base:

Combine base ingredients in a food processor. Process until breadcrumbs begin to stick together. Do not over process. Lightly grease a fluted edge pie dish and press crumbs firmly over base and sides. Cook at 180°C for 15 minutes.

To make filling:

Spread zucchini over base. Top with slices of tomato. Sprinkle over basil and oregano. Add mushrooms. Beat egg whites and milk. Add parsley and pour over mushrooms. Spoon yoghurt in a circle over mushrooms. Sprinkle cheese over yoghurt. Sprinkle over breadcrumbs. Cook at 200°C for 40 to 50 minutes.

mousse – beetroot

500g cooked beetroot (roughly
   chopped)
1 tbsp wine vinegar
¾ cup non-fat yoghurt

1 tbsp unsweetened orange juice
1 tbsp gelatine
¼ cup boiling water
2 egg whites

Purée the first three ingredients in a blender, until smooth. Dissolve gelatine in boiling water. Add to beetroot. Add yoghurt. Beat egg whites until stiff. Gently fold through until just combined. Pour into a mould and refrigerate until quite firm. Slice and serve with salads.

mousse – fresh tomato

serves 4–6

1 kg ripe tomatoes
2 tbsps gelatine
½ cup boiling water
1 egg white
1 cup non-fat yoghurt
2 tbsps tomato paste (salt and
sugar free)

2 tbsps finely chopped red
capsicum
2 tbsps finely grated cucumber
2 tbsps finely chopped fresh herbs
(mixed) (parsley, basil, oregano)

Pour boiling water over tomatoes and leave to stand until skins begin to break (approximately 3–5 minutes). Drain. Peel. Cut in half and scoop out as many seeds as possible. Pour boiling water over gelatine and stir to dissolve. Leave to cool slightly. Place tomatoes and tomato paste in a blender and purée until smooth. Add gelatine and then the yoghurt. Fold through the red capsicum, grated cucumber and herbs. Beat egg white until stiff. Fold through mixture until just combined. Pour into individual moulds and refrigerate until quite firm.

mousse – salmon

serves 8

450g red salmon (lightly cooked,
salt free)
¼ cup lemon juice
¼ cup boiling water
1 tbsp dijon mustard
¼ cup finely chopped celery
¼ cup cider vinegar

1 tbsp gelatine
1 cup non-fat yoghurt
¼ cup finely chopped green
capsicum
1 tbsp finely grated fresh
horseradish (optional)

Combine salmon, vinegar and lemon juice in a food processor and lightly puree. Dissolve gelatine in boiling water. Add yoghurt and mustard to salmon and puree to combine. Add gelatine and mix well. Fold through the remaining ingredients and pour into a glass mould. Refrigerate until quite firm. Serve with salad.

open vegetable pie

serves 8

We share this meal often with Mum and Dad. It is never the same pie twice, and it's amazing I actually got Mum to remember the ingredients! It really just depends what vegetables are at hand and depending on which herb bush looks the healthiest at the time of making the pie. Let your imagination run wild and create many variations of this wonderful wholesome pie.

pita bread
500g mince steak (fat free)
1 medium onion, finely chopped
2 large potatoes, grated
1 zucchini, grated
200g pumpkin, grated
1 clove garlic, finely chopped

1 medium carrot, grated
2 tbsps finely chopped parsley
1 teaspoon oregano
1 cup chopped celery
2 egg whites
1½ cups wholemeal breadcrumbs
½ cup finely chopped celery leaves

Line a 30cm pie plate with pita bread. Cook meat in 1 tablespoon water, stir and cook for 5 minutes. Add meat to prepared vegetables. Stir well. Add egg whites and stir thoroughly. Press into lined plate. Top with breadcrumbs and celery leaves.

Cook in moderate oven at 180°C for 1 hour.

pastie vegetable roll

makes 3 rolls, serves 9

500g chopped leeks or onions
1 clove garlic, crushed
3 medium potatoes
450g grated pumpkin
125g grated parsnip
6 green beans, chopped
¼ small cabbage, finely chopped
1 large zucchini, grated

6 medium mushrooms, sliced
½ medium red pepper
1 stick celery, chopped
2 granny smith apples, peeled and
   grated
9 sheets of wholemeal filo pastry
¼ cup fresh chopped herbs
   (optional)

Cook leeks and garlic for 2 minutes in 2 tablespoons of water. Combine with all other ingredients and mix well. Drain off any juices.

Lay filo pastry as illustrated in the diagram. Use 3 sheets of pastry for each roll. Lay one sheet on top of the other and the third sheet should cover the top ¼ of these. Place ⅓ of the mixture as shown in the diagram. Fold sides in and roll the bottom end to the top. Repeat.

Place on a lightly greased large non-stick baking tray. Cook at 190°C for 1¼ hours.

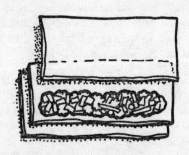

potato and pumpkin layer pie

serves 8

Base:

2 cups wholemeal breadcrumbs

2 tbsps unsweetened orange juice

Layers:

1kg potatoes, peeled, cooked and mashed

2 granny smith apples, peeled and grated

½ cup spring onions, chopped

dash of cayenne pepper

1 cup cooked peas

800g pumpkin, peeled, cooked and mashed

¼ cup tomato chutney spread

1 small red capsicum, thinly sliced

1 large tomato, sliced

1 cup wholemeal breadcrumbs

To make base:

Combine base ingredients in a food processor until crumbs begin to stick together. Press into a round springform cheese cake tin, that has been lightly greased. Cook at 200°C for 10 minutes. Remove from oven. Leave to cool.

To make layers:

Combine mashed potato, apple, spring onions, peas and cayenne pepper. Mix well. Spoon over base and firm down. Combine pumpkin, tomato chutney spread and capsicum. Spread over potato mixture and firm down. Top with slices of tomato, then breadcrumbs.

Cook at 200°C for 50 minutes. Let stand for 10 minutes before removing from the tin. Slice with an electric knife or very sharp knife.

potato kebabs

serves 2

Kebabs:
6 medium potatoes

1 long leek

Sauce:
2 cloves garlic, crushed

1 granny smith apple, peeled and grated

400g fresh tomatoes, peeled and seeded

1 cup grated carrot

1 tbsp fresh basil, finely chopped

1 tbsp fresh rosemary, finely chopped

¼ cup tomato paste

To make kebabs:
Peel potatoes. Cut the white part of the leek into 4. Cut each piece in half (opposite direction). Thread the potato and leek onto a kebab skewer.

Place in oven bag or wrap in foil and cook at 200°C for 40 minutes or until potatoes are tender. Remove from bag. Position on a serving plate and pour over sauce.

To make sauce:
Place garlic in a small saucepan with 2 tablespoons of water. Cover and cook gently for 2 minutes. Add apple. Cook for 2 minutes further, and add all other ingredients. Cover and simmer on low heat for 30 minutes.

potato vegetable mound

serves 6–8

1kg cooked potatoes
3 cups wholemeal breadcrumbs
2 tbsps finely grated low fat grating
cheese
½ cup grated carrot
½ cup cooked peas
½ cup grated zucchini

½ cup chopped parsley
½ cup chopped spring onions
½–1 teaspoon dill
1 egg white
1 egg white (extra)
2 cups wholemeal breadcrumbs
½ cup finely chopped celery leaves

Drain potatoes and mash lightly. Combine all the ingredients except the extra egg white, breadcrumbs and celery, and mix well. Line an oven tray with foil and grease lightly. Sprinkle over some wholemeal flour or wholemeal breadcrumbs. Place the potato vegetable mixture on top and using a spatula, shape into a mound.

Beat extra egg white lightly and brush over the potato. Sprinkle over remaining combined breadcrumbs and celery. Press down evenly.

Cook at 180°C for 20 minutes or until breadcrumbs are browned. Serve as a side dish or with salads.

potted meat

500g cooked lamb shank meat,
chopped with all fat removed
(use meat from lamb shank
stock)
2 granny smith apples, peeled and
chopped into small cubes

2 cups lamb shank stock
3 teaspoons gelatine
½ teaspoon finely ground nutmeg
1 teaspoon dried basil
1 tbsp finely chopped parsley

Place the lamb shank meat into a deep ceramic or china bowl (approximately 3½ to 4 cups). Cook the apple in the stock for 2 minutes. Add gelatine and stir to dissolve. Remove from heat. Add spices and parsley. Pour over meat. Set aside to cool and refrigerate. Serve with salads, allowing 2 slices per person.

pumpkin and tomato quiche

serves 6–8

Base:

4 sheets wholemeal filo pastry

Filling:

700g cooked pumpkin
1 cup low fat evaporated skim milk
1 cup finely chopped shallots
½ cup finely chopped parsley
4 egg whites

black ground pepper to taste
  (optional)
1 teaspoon of curry powder
2 medium tomatoes

Lightly grease a 30cm quiche flan. Place pastry sheets (one on top of the other) in flan. Neaten around edges. Place pumpkin and evaporated milk in a blender and process until smooth. Add shallots, parsley and stir through lightly beaten egg whites. Add pepper or curry powder. Pour over pastry. Slice tomatoes thinly and place over the top of pie.

Cook at 180° for 60 minutes or until firm.

quick spinach and mushroom pizza

serves 2

1 large wholemeal pita bread
¼ cup low fat ricotta cheese
2 large tomatoes
1 cup pizza tomato sauce (see below)

½ cup finely chopped spinach
2 cups finely sliced mushrooms
2 tbsps finely grated low fat cheese
¼ cup wholemeal breadcrumbs

Pizza Tomato Sauce:

1 onion
2 cloves garlic, crushed
2 large tomatoes, peeled and
  chopped

1 tbsp tomato paste
½–1 teaspoon oregano
½–1 teaspoon basil
¼ cup water

To make sauce:
Combine all ingredients. Cook for 10 minutes covered. Remove lid. Cook until reduced and thickened.

To make pizza:
Spread pita bread with ricotta cheese. Top with slices of tomato. Mix mushrooms and spinach in pizza tomato sauce and pour over tomatoes. Sprinkle over combined cheese and breadcrumbs. Cook in a hot oven for 10 minutes. Serve with a salad.

ratatouille

serves 4

½ cup stock/water
2 white onions, cut into wedges (cut in half, in half again and repeat until wedges are small enough)
2 cloves garlic, crushed
2 egg plants, coarsely chopped
2 zucchini, sliced
4 tomatoes, peeled and chopped

2 capsicums, chopped
6 green beans, chopped
1 stick celery, chopped
10 cauliflower flowerettes
1 carrot, thinly sliced
1 teaspoon dried basil and
1 teaspoon celery seed

In a large frying pan add stock, onions and garlic. Cover and cook for 2 minutes over a gentle heat. Add egg plant and zucchini, cook for 5 minutes. Add tomatoes and all other ingredients. Sprinkle over herbs. Move around the pan for 10 minutes. Serve on a bed of brown rice or wholemeal toast.

rice mould

serves 8–10

3 cups brown rice
1 cup peas
1 cup grated carrot
½ cup green capsicum, finely chopped
½ cup red capsicum, finely chopped
1 cup alfalfa sprouts

1 cup spring onions
1 cup celery
½ cup cucumber, peeled, seeded and chopped
½ cup fresh chopped herbs
2 tbsps garlic vinaigrette
½ cup cooked puréed apple
¼ teaspoon cayenne pepper

Cook rice in boiling water for 20 minutes. Add peas and cook for a further 5 minutes. Drain. Set aside to cool slightly. Combine all other ingredients and mix well while rice is still warm. Lightly grease a deep mould and firmly press rice mixture in. Press down firmly around the top. Cover with foil and refrigerate at least 4 hours prior to serving.

Serve a slice on a bed of lettuce with chunks of fresh pineapple and cherry tomatoes.

roast of turkey breast

serves 10

1kg breast of turkey (fat removed)
1 clove garlic, crushed
2 tbsps finely chopped onion
1½ tbsps orange juice
  (unsweetened)
1 cup wholemeal breadcrumbs
6 medium mushrooms, sliced thinly

2 spring onions, finely chopped
¼ teaspoon sage
½ teaspoon marjoram
2 medium carrots (cut into very thin
  circles)
1½ cups water

Gravy:

1 tbsp tomato paste

2 tbsps cornflour

Crunchy Baked Mushrooms:

20 medium mushrooms
20 tbsps non-fat cottage cheese

½ cup wholemeal breadcrumbs

Roast:

Cook the garlic and onion in the orange juice for 3 minutes until onion is soft. Add to the breadcrumbs, mushrooms, spring onions and spices. Mix well.

Cut a pocket into the turkey breast. Fill the pocket with the mushroom, breadcrumb mixture. Secure with skewers.

In a baking dish, line the base with the carrot. Add the water. Lie the turkey breast on top. Cover with foil. Baste turkey every 15 minutes. Cook at 180°C for 1 hour.

Serve with dry baked potato, steamed carrots, peas and crunchy baked mushrooms.

Gravy:

Remove turkey from baking dish. Place juices and carrot in a blender. Add tomato paste. Blend until smooth. Pour into a saucepan and slowly bring to the boil. Make a paste with the cornflour and a small amount of water. Stir into the gravy to thicken. Spoon over the turkey slices.

Crunchy Baked Mushrooms:

Allow 2 mushrooms per person. Peel and remove two stems. Top with a spoonful of cottage cheese and sprinkle over generously with wholemeal breadcrumbs. Cook at 200°C for 10 minutes or until well browned.

spinach and vegetable terrine

serves 6

4 cups finely chopped spinach	1 cup finely chopped leek
2 cups chopped cooked baby carrots	4 egg whites
	1 cup non-fat yoghurt
2 cups cooked potato cubes	1 teaspoon nutmeg

Place spinach in a food processor and using the chopping blade, process until spinach is very fine (4 cups). Combine spinach, carrots, potato and leek. Lightly beat egg whites and yoghurt and pour over. Add nutmeg. Mix together without breaking up cooked vegetables. Press firmly into a glass or ceramic terrine. Cover with foil.

Place in a water bath and cook at 180°C for 1 hour. Remove from oven and let stand for 10 minutes before slicing. (Excellent, hot or cold.)

spinach and zucchini slice

serves 6

Base:

2 cups wholemeal breadcrumbs	1 tbsp unsweetened orange juice

Filling:

100g finely chopped spinach/silver beet, green part only	200g finely chopped leeks
	1 cup low fat ricotta cheese
400g grated zucchini	2 egg whites
2 granny smith apples, peeled and grated	1 teaspoon nutmeg

Topping:

2 cups wholemeal breadcrumbs

To make base:

Combine breadcrumbs and orange juice in a food processor. Process until breadcrumbs look moist and begin to stick to each other. Line a 20cm × 30cm slice tin with foil. Lightly grease. Press crumb mixture firmly onto the bottom of the tin. Cook at 200°C for 10 minutes.

To make filling:

Combine all ingredients in a large bowl and mix thoroughly (hands are best). Spread evenly over base and press down firmly.

Spread breadcrumbs over filling and again, press down firmly with your hand. Cook at 200°C for 50 minutes.

spinach chicken drumsticks in wholemeal filo pastry

serves 8

8 chicken drumsticks (approx 90g
    each), skin removed
8 pieces wholemeal filo pastry
1 cup very finely minced fresh
    spinach or silver beet leaves
1 cup ricotta cheese
½ lemon – juice of
black pepper to taste

Cabbage and Spinach Salad:
1 cup finely minced spinach
¼ cabbage finely minced
2 carrots finely minced
1 cup alfalfa sprouts
black pepper
Dressing: ½ cup mayonnaise (see
    Dressings section)

To prepare drumsticks:
Combine the black pepper, lemon juice, ricotta cheese and spinach or silver beet and mix well.

Take a good heaped tablespoonful of the mixture and press around the chicken drumstick. Fold a sheet of pastry in half. Place chicken drumstick on pastry sheet and roll up. Place on a baking tray.

Repeat with remaining ingredients and cook at 200°C for 50 to 60 minutes.

Serve with Cabbage and Spinach Salad and a basket of wholemeal rolls.

Salad:
Mix all ingredients well.

spinach lasagne slice

Take approximately 24 sheets spinach lasagne noodles (made from semolina and spinach).

Vegetable Sauce:
2 cloves garlic
½ cup thinly sliced celery
1 cup green beans (top and tail,
    and cut into small pieces)
1 cup zucchini (top and tail, cut
    into thin rounds and then into 4)

1 cup carrot (wash, cut into thin
    rounds and roughly chop into
    small pieces)
1 cup red capsicum (cut in half and
    remove seeds, cut into strips and
    roughly chop into small pieces)

1 teaspoon dried oregano
1 teaspoon dried rosemary
800g cooked tomatoes and juice
300g fresh spinach or silver beet
    leaves
2 small onions

½ cup thinly sliced mushrooms
1 teaspoon dried basil
1½ cup water/dry white wine
⅓ cup tomato paste (salt free and
    sugar free)

White sauce:
2 cups soy milk
4 tbsps cornflour

2 bay leaves
100g low fat grating cheese

Drop lasagne noodles one at a time into a large pan of boiling water. Add ½ cup lemon to the boiling water. As noodles cook remove and drop into chilled water. Leave here until required. Drain well before using. (You could also use the Instant Noodle variety which need no prior cooking.)

Crush garlic and chop onions finely. Cook gently with a small amount of water, with the lid on for 3 minutes. Add all the vegetables and herbs and pour over the water or wine. Replace lid and cook for 10 minutes. Add tomatoes and juice. Leave lid off and let bubble for 20 minutes. Add tomato paste and cook for a further 10 minutes. Stir occasionally so that the vegetables do not stick to the bottom of the pan. Remove from heat.

Place spinach or silver beet leaves in a saucepan with boiling water and cook for 2 minutes. Drain well.

Place 1¾ cups soy milk and bay leaves in a saucepan. Slowly bring to the boil. Mix remaining soy milk with cornflour to make a paste. Stir through the milk briskly before it comes to the boil. Stir all the time while sauce thickens (approximately 2 minutes). Place a layer of noodles in the bottom of a large lasagne dish. Pour over some vegetable sauce and top with a layer of noodles. Pour over half of remaining vegetable sauce, top with spinach and half the white sauce, and top with another layer of noodles. Pour over remaining sauce, top with noodles. Spread remaining white sauce evenly over the top layer of noodles and sprinkle with the grated cheese.

spinach pancakes with lobster filling

makes 8 (large)

2 cups wholemeal plain flour
1/4 cup finely chopped spinach
1/4 cup skim milk powder

2 1/2 cups water
2 egg whites

Lobster filling:
Allow 90g lobster meat per person

Sauce:

2 cups skim milk
3–4 tbsps cornflour
1 tbsp tomato paste
2 teaspoons dijon mustard

2 tbsps grated low fat cheese
black ground pepper or a squeeze of
   lemon juice to taste (optional)

To make pancakes:
Combine all ingredients in a blender and process until smooth. Leave to stand for 30 minutes before using. Lightly grease a non-stick pancake pan, and pour small amounts onto pan and spread over evenly. Cook for 3 minutes one side or until air bubbles appear. Turn and cook for 2 minutes. Keep warm.

To make sauce:
Slowly bring 1 3/4 cups of milk to the boil. Combine 1/4 cup milk, cornflour, tomato paste and dijon mustard and mix well. Stir into boiling milk and stir thoroughly until thickened (add more cornflour if you desire a thicker sauce). Add cheese, pepper or lemon.

Fill pancakes with lobster and pour over sauce before rolling.

stuffed marrows

serves 2

1 medium sized marrow
1 large onion, finely chopped
1 clove garlic, crushed
125g minced beef (fat free)
100g carrot, grated
150g cabbage, finely chopped
50g parsnip, grated

50g peas
2 tbsps finely chopped parsley
1/2 cup mushrooms, thinly sliced
2 tbsps water
1 cup skim milk
1 tbsp cornflour
1/2 cup wholemeal breadcrumbs

Cut a slice from the marrow, lengthways. Scoop out the seeds. Cook onion and garlic in a small amount of water until tender and transparent, add meat and cook for 10 minutes, stir to break meat up. Add carrot, cabbage, parsnip and peas. Cover and cook for further 3 minutes. Add parsley and remove from heat. Cook mushrooms in water, covered for 5 minutes on a low heat. Add ¾ cup milk. Slowly bring to the boil. Combine ¼ cup milk and cornflour and stir through milk and mushrooms. Stir until thickened. Spoon meat and vegetable mixture into marrow and pour over mushroom sauce. Sprinkle over breadcrumbs.

Bake in a non-stick oven dish for 25 minutes at 180°C. Cut in half. Serve with salads.

tomato and rice slice with rosemary

serves 6

Crust:
1 cup cooked wholemeal brown rice (keep warm)

2 egg whites

Filling:
½ cup water
1 onion
1 cup chopped celery
1 medium zucchini, thinly sliced
1 cup chopped green beans
1 small green capsicum, cut in half, seeds removed and thinly sliced

3 medium carrots, thinly sliced
400g tomatoes (bottled) and juice
1 teaspoon dried oregano
1 teaspoon dried rosemary
2 tbsps tomato paste
2 tbsps arrowroot to thicken

Topping:
2 cups wholemeal bread cubes
¼ cup low fat grating cheese
½–1 teaspoon garlic powder (optional)

To make crust:
Combine cooked rice and egg white. Spread into a lightly greased ovenproof dish, and smooth down.

To make filling:
In a saucepan, combine the first 7 ingredients. Simmer over a gentle heat for 5 minutes. Add remaining ingredients and cook for a further 10 minutes. Pour over rice.

To make topping:
Combine topping ingredients and spread over filling. Cook at 200°C for 30 minutes.

tuna curry slice

serves 6

Base:
2 cups wholemeal breadcrumbs

Filling:
400g lightly cooked tuna
1 cup finely sliced celery
1 cup grated apple
¼ cup finely chopped chives
2 tbsps wholemeal plain flour
½ cup skim milk

½ cup unsweetened apple juice
3 egg whites
2–3 teaspoons curry powder
2 cups mashed potato (whipped)
2 tbsps finely grated low fat grating
   cheese

To make base:
Toast breadcrumbs until brown and crisp. Lightly grease a 20cm × 30cm deep rectangular baking dish and line with foil. Press crumbs onto the base of dish while still hot. Set aside.

To make filling:
Combine tuna, celery, apple and chives and spread over the base. Place flour in a saucepan and heat for a few seconds. Add milk and stir briskly. Add apple juice and stir until sauce thickens. Beat egg whites lightly and stir through sauce (remove from heat first). Add curry powder to taste. Cook for 2 minutes. Pour over tuna. Combine whipped potato with cheese and spread evenly over tuna. Press down with a fork. Cook for 30 to 40 minutes or until the top is browned at 180°C.

tuna pitas

serves 4

This is a quick and easy lunch idea or Sunday night easy tea.

180g tuna (water packed) or salmon
  (water packed)
2 small zucchini, grated
8 spring onions, finely chopped
6 medium mushrooms, finely sliced
2 stalks celery, thinly sliced
1 small green pepper, finely
  chopped

2 medium carrots, grated
100g low fat grating cheese, grated
1 teaspoon oregano (dried)
1 tbsp lemon balm (fresh), finely
  chopped
2 tomatoes
4 large pita bread

Drain tuna/salmon. Combine all ingredients except tomatoes and bread and mix well.

Cut tomatoes into 16 slices. Place 4 slices of tomato in a row across each pita bread.

Divide mixture into four equal amounts and place on each of the pita breads over the tomatoes. Roll up firmly and place on a lightly greased baking tray.

Cook at 200°C for 25 minutes.

tuna potato roulade

serves 6–8

1kg peeled potatoes
¼ cup chopped spring onions
  (green part only)

3 cups wholemeal breadcrumbs
1 egg white

Filling:

200g tuna (water packed)
1 cup chopped spring onions (green
  part only)
1 granny smith apple, peeled and
  cut in quarters

10 medium mushroom, washed
1 tbsp lemon juice

Steam potatoes lightly until tender; drain and mash. Fold in ¼ cup spring onions, breadcrumbs and egg white and mix well. Place a sheet of foil on a baking tray (approximately 30cm × 33cm). Lightly grease and sprinkle over wholemeal plain flour. While potato is still warm, spoon it in 'blobs' over the baking tray. Flatten down with the palm of your hand until flat (approximately 1cm thick).

94

Combine filling mixture in a food processor and using the stop start button lightly process. Spoon filling mixture along one edge of the longest side of foil. Press down firmly. Pick up the end of the foil at the same edge and begin to roll over. (If filling starts to fall, just keep pressing it back into position with your hand). Keep rolling until there is no more potato. Use a knife or spatula to flatten edge onto the main roll to make an even finish.

Place carefully on a lightly greased baking tray. Cook in a hot oven 250°C for 30 minutes, turn heat down and cook for a further 30 minutes at 200°C.

Serve with lightly steamed julienne of vegetables in season. For example, carrot, celery, zucchini, yellow zucchini, cucumber, spring onions.

turkey drumsticks

serves 4

4 medium turkey drumsticks (remove skins)
125g wholemeal bread (break into small pieces)
4 medium mushrooms (peel and cut into 4)

2 tbsps finely chopped onion
1 clove garlic, crushed
1½ tbsps unsweetened orange juice
1 egg white and 1 tbsp water
wholemeal plain flour

Combine bread and mushrooms in a food processor. Process until lightly crumbed (be careful not to over process, as the mushrooms add moisture to the bread and can tend to make the crumbs sticky). Cook onions and garlic in orange juice for 3 minutes until onions are soft. Combine breadcrumb mixture and onions.

Roll the turkey drumstick in flour, then in the beaten egg white. Roll in the breadcrumb mixture. Repeat with remaining drumsticks. Place in an oven bag. Seal. Prick bag to make two small holes.

Cook at 180°C for 40 to 50 minutes. Remove from oven bag and leave to cool. Refrigerate. Serve with salads.

veal and mushroom burger with cabbage, onion and cucumber salad

serves 6

Burger:

500g veal

1–2 cloves garlic

2 medium onions

200g mushrooms

¼ cup wholemeal plain flour

1 egg white

good squeeze of lemon juice

Salad:

2 cups finely chopped cabbage

½ cup finely chopped spring onions

½ cup grated cucumber

¼ cup mayonnaise

Burger:

Chop veal into small pieces. Crush garlic. Chop onions roughly. Peel and wash mushrooms and chop roughly.

Place veal, garlic and onions into a food processor and process until finely minced. Add mushrooms and process until mushrooms are finely chopped and combined. Add flour, egg white and lemon juice. Mix well. Shape into 6 balls.

Place on a non-stick frying pan and cook on a low heat. Flatten veal balls down. Cook for 2 minutes one side and turn. Cook a further 2 minutes.

Serve on wholemeal bread rolls, lightly toasted, with cabbage, onion and cucumber salad, on top of burger.

Salad:

Mix all ingredients well.

vegetable flan

serves 6

400g grated potato

400g grated carrot

200g grated zucchini

1 small onion, peeled and chopped

1 clove garlic, crushed

½ cup finely minced spinach

1 cup breadcrumbs

2 tbsps skim milk powder

½ teaspoon curry powder

2 egg whites

¼ cup non-fat yoghurt

1 cup finely chopped parsley

Combine all ingredients and mix well. Spoon into a lightly greased ovenproof dish. Cook for 1 hour at 200°C. Cover with foil for first 40 minutes, remove foil for last 20 minutes.

vegetable shepherd's pie

serves 6

This is an adaption of one of my favourite meals as a child. You could use any vegetable combination depending on what's in season or more importantly what's in your vegetable tray at the time of making it.

Vegetables:

2 medium carrots, peeled and cubed
1 potato, peeled and cubed
12 brussel sprouts, cut in half
1 medium zucchini, cut into slices
150g cauliflower flowerettes

150g broccoli flowerettes
¾ cup green beans, cut into small pieces
100g pumpkin, peeled and cubed
½ cup grated parsnip
100g chopped cabbage

Place all vegetables in the top of a steamer and lightly steam for 12 minutes.

Gravy:

1 onion, peeled and sliced
2 cloves garlic, crushed
2 cups vegetable/chicken stock
1 tbsp tomato paste

2 tbsps cornflour
2 tbsps water
¼–½ cup chopped parsley

Sauté onion and garlic in 2 tablespoons of stock for 2 minutes. Add stock and stir in tomato paste. Combine cornflour and water to make a paste. As the gravy begins to bubble, stir cornflour paste into it. Add parsley. Cook for 5 minutes on a low heat, stirring continuously. Spoon vegetables into a suitable casserole or baking dish. Spoon over the gravy.

Topping:

3–4 cups hot mashed potato (approximately 8 medium potatoes)

Spread the potato over the vegetables and gravy evenly by using a fork (this will give an interesting effect to the top of the pie, once it is cooked). Place in a water bath and cook at 230°C for 40 minutes.

vegetable terrine

serves 8 as an entrée
serves 4 as a meal

Spinach layer:
12 spinach leaves
1 clove crushed garlic
½ cup non-fat yoghurt

1 tbsp skim milk powder
3 egg whites

Potato Layer
250g mashed potato
1 cup finely chopped spring onions
  (white part only)

2 tbsps non-fat yoghurt
2 egg whites

Carrot layer:
500g cooked baby carrots
½ cup non-fat yoghurt
2 tbsps tomato paste

3 egg whites

Wash spinach and remove white stalks. Chop spinach finely. Place in a saucepan with garlic and cook in a small amount of water for 3 minutes. Drain. Process spinach in a food processor until smooth. Stir in yoghurt, skim milk and eggs. Process again until all ingredients are combined.

Pour spinach mixture into a lightly greased 25cm × 15cm terrine. Cover with foil. Place in a water bath. Water should come half way up terrine. Cook at 180°C for 30 minutes. Remove from oven and remove foil.

Combine ingredients for potato layer and spoon over the spinach layer. Cover, return to the oven and cook for 30 minutes at 180°C. Remove from the oven and remove foil.

Place carrot layer ingredients in a food processor and process until smooth. Pour over potato layer, cover with foil, return to the oven and cook for a further 30 minutes.

Remove from oven, remove foil and let stand for 10 minutes before turning out to serve hot. If using as a cold dish, leave in terrine until cold and refrigerate.

As an entrée serve with crisp julienne strips of vegetables.

white fish with lemon sauce

serves 6

500g fish fillets
2 cups cooked mashed potato
2 granny smith apples, peeled and
    grated
1 egg white
½ cup finely chopped spring onions
    (white part only)

1 tbsp finely chopped basil (fresh)
2 tbsps finely chopped oregano
    (fresh)
¼ cup non-fat yoghurt

Lemon Sauce:

½ cup lemon juice
½ cup unsweetened orange juice

1 tbsp apple juice concentrate
2 tbsps arrowroot

Brown Parsley Rice:

3 cups cooked brown rice (hot)

1 cup chopped parsley

Tomato, Onion and Cucumber in Herb Vinaigrette:

24 cherry tomatoes
2 odourless onions, peeled and cut
    into thin wedges

1 cucumber, cut in half, seeds
    removed and sliced thinly to
    make a ½ moon shape.
1 cup herb vinaigrette (see
    Dressings section)

To cook fish:

Chop fish fillets into small pieces. Combine with all other ingredients. Lightly grease a mould (preferably a fish shape mould).
Spoon mixture into mould and pack down firmly. Place in a water
bath and cover with foil. Cook at 180°C for 30 minutes.

To make vegetable salad:

Combine all ingredients and pour over 1 cup of herb vinaigrette.

Lemon Sauce:

Combine all ingredients. Stir over heat until sauce boils and thickens.
Serve over the fish.

whole baked pumpkin with sage and onion stuffing

serves 8

1 × 1½–2kg pumpkin
1 large onion or the white part of 25 small leeks
2 cups wholemeal breadcrumbs, toasted
¼ teaspoon nutmeg
black ground pepper to taste (optional)

1 sage leaf
good handful of finely chopped parsley
1 cup finely grated low fat cheese
1½ cups water
1 bay leaf

Cut a lid from the top of the pumpkin and set aside. Scrape out the seeds and stringy bits and a small part of the flesh. Place on a baking tray. Cook onion/leek in a small amount of water until soft and transparent. Add to breadcrumbs with nutmeg, pepper, chopped sage, parsley and cheese. Combine well. Pack stuffing into pumpkin. Pour in the liquid. Top with the bay leaf. Wrap pumpkin lid in foil. Place on top of pumpkin and cook at 180°C for 2 hours.

To serve, cut into wedges with a sharp knife or an electric knife and serve with a selection of salads.

rice

Brown Rice is the natural unpolished rice that has been hulled but still has its bran. It has a nutty flavour and is extremely nutritious. It takes longer to cook than white rice, and it is nearly impossible to overcook it. Never cook rice to the extent that it becomes claggy – it should always have a little 'bite' about it.

I have only recently discovered Wild Rice – actually it is an acquatic grass grown in North America, but very much resembles rice in its shape and texture. It is expensive but its flavour is more intensely nutty than brown rice and worth having on the table once or twice a year.

When we were first married rice was forbidden in any shape or form, as Bruce had been served a 'scoop' of white rice at Boarding School for 5 years with the main meal, and made to eat it. I was unaware at the time that brown rice or wild rice existed. However, I might add that brown rice is very much a family favourite now.

Sometimes it is served along with other dishes, or it is a meal on its own. Here are some of our favourites.

carrot and cummin rice

serves 4

4 cups cooked brown rice
2 cups grated raw carrot
½ cup currants
½ cup finely chopped spring onions
½–1 teaspoon cummin
½–1 teaspoon ginger powder
¼ cup unsweetened pineapple juice

Combine all ingredients and mix well. Serve.

chilli rice

serves 4

4 cups cooked brown rice
4 egg whites
½ cup soy milk
1 cup finely chopped celery
½ cup finely chopped spring onion
1 small green capsicum, cut in
  strips

1 small red capsicum, cut in strips
½ teaspoon dried basil
½ teaspoon ginger powder
½ teaspoon turmeric
½–1 teaspoon chilli powder
½ cup stock

Beat egg whites and soy milk. Very lightly grease a non-stick pan. Place pan over heat to get moderately hot. Pour over egg white mixture and let cook until it sets. Turn, cook other side. Remove from heat and slice thinly. Add celery, onion, capsicums, and spices to pan with stock. Cook for 2 minutes on high or until all moisture is absorbed. Add rice. Turn off heat. Toss rice through, to just warm. Add sliced egg white and serve.

garlic rice

serves 4

2 cups raw brown rice
3 cloves garlic (crushed)
1 large onion peeled and finely
  chopped

1 granny smith apple, peeled and
  grated
6 cups of stock or water

Cook garlic and onion in 2 tbsps stock until soft and transparent. Add apple and cook a further 2 minutes on a gentle heat, stirring constantly. Add remaining stock and rice. Cover and cook over a gentle heat until all moisture is absorbed or rice is soft.

ginger rice

serves 4

2 cups raw brown rice
2 teaspoons finely chopped ginger
  root
1 tbsp ginger root juice (obtain by

placing small pieces of ginger
  root in a garlic press)
6 cups of water or stock

Cook finely chopped ginger and juice with ¼ cup water or stock for 3 minutes. Add rice and remaining liquid. Cook until rice is soft. Serve.

lemon herbed rice

serves 4

4 cups cooked brown rice
1 cup of mixed fresh finely chopped
    herbs (parsley, chives, basil,
    oregano, tarragon, thyme etc.)

2 tbsps tarragon vinegar
2 teaspoons lemon juice
2 teaspoons lemon zest

Combine all ingredients and mix well. Serve.

mushroom rice

serves 6

4 cups brown rice
1 cup cooked wild rice
2 cups thinly sliced mushrooms
1 small green capsicum, cut into
    thin strips
½ cup finely chopped spring onions

2 tbsps finely chopped fresh basil
2 tbsps finely chopped fresh
    oregano
fresh ground black pepper to taste
2 tbsps cider vinegar
2 tbsps lemon juice

Combine all ingredients and mix well. Chill. Serve.

pineapple rice

serves 2

2 cups cooked brown rice
1 cup pineapple pieces
    (unsweetened)
1 small zucchini cut into thin
    rounds

3 tbsps finely chopped lemon balm
¼ cup unsweetened pineapple juice

Combine all ingredients and mix well. Chill. Serve.

rice combination

serves 4

2 cups cooked brown rice
2 cups cooked wild rice
1 cup finely chopped celery
½ cup finely chopped onion

2 tbsps finely chopped garlic chives
2 tbsps finely chopped fresh basil
¼ cup vinaigrette

Combine all ingredients and mix well. Refrigerate for at least 1 hour
before serving. Serve.

saffron rice

serves 2

1 cup raw long grain brown rice
2½ cups defatted chicken stock
pinch of saffron

1 teaspoon lemon zest
¼–½ teaspoon cinnamon

Bring stock to the boil and simmer. Add saffron. Leave for 3 minutes. Add rice. Cover and cook until soft but still slightly 'bitey', and rice has absorbed the colour and flavour of the saffron. Add lemon zest and cinnamon. Mix well. Serve.

spinach rice

serves 2

2 cups cooked brown rice
½ cup cooked green peas
½–1 finely chopped spinach or
  silverbeet leaves (white stems
  removed)

½ cup finely chopped spring onions
¼ cup finely chopped parsley
2 tbsps finely chopped mint
¼ cup vinaigrette dressing

Combine all ingredients and mix well. Chill. Serve.

sweet rice

serves 4

4 cups cooked brown rice
¼ cup finely chopped dried apricots
¼ cup currants
¼ cup finely chopped raisins
¼ cup finely chopped dried apples

1 medium green capsicum
1 cup finely chopped celery
1 teaspoon mixed spice
2 teaspoons orange rind zest
¼ cup unsweetened orange juice

Combine all ingredients and mix well. Chill. Serve.

tabbouleh rice

serves 6

2 cups cooked brown rice
4 tomatoes, peeled, seeded and finely
  chopped
4 spring onions finely chopped

1 cup finely chopped parsley
1 cup finely chopped fresh coriander
½ cup finely chopped fresh mint
¾ cup garlic vinaigrette

Combine all ingredients and mix well. Chill and serve.

perfect desserts

Perfect desserts are fruit desserts – either one fruit or a combination of fruits with very little fuss. Choose from what fruit is in season and dress it up just a little.

almond oranges

serves 6

8 oranges
1 cup unsweetened orange juice
finely grated rind of 1 orange
  (preferably in long thin strips)

12 almonds, in the skins

Using a sharp knife, pare off the peel and pith from oranges. To cut segments, cut on either side of the membrane and remove segments. Combine all ingredients in a pan and simmer gently for 20 minutes. Leave to cool. Remove almonds. Refrigerate.
  Serve chilled.

apple and carrot pie

serves 8

Base:

1½ cups wholemeal breadcrumbs
1 teaspoon cinnamon

2 tbsps orange juice

Filling:

500g cooked apple chunks
finely grated rind of 1 lemon
finely grated rind of 1 orange
½ cup of chopped raisins

½ cup unsweetened orange juice
1 teaspoon arrowroot
2 teaspoons water
½ cup grated raw carrot

Topping:

¼ cup untoasted muesli (sugar and salt free) remove all dried fruit

1 teaspoon cinnamon

To make base:

Combine breadcrumbs, cinnamon and orange juice in a food processor and lightly process until crumbs begin to stick together. Do not over process. Line a 20cm round cake tin with foil. Lightly grease the base. Press breadcrumb mixture firmly over the base. Cook for 10 minutes at 180°C. Remove from oven and cool. Turn oven up to 200°C.

To make filling:

Combine apple, lemon rind, orange rind, raisins and orange juice, in a saucepan. Slowly bring to the boil. As bubbles appear, combine arrowroot and water and stir in. Take off heat and fold in carrot. Pour apple mixture over the base and sprinkle over muesli and cinnamon. Cook for 30 minutes at 200°C.

apple snow

serves 2

2 crisp apples

1 passionfruit

Place unpeeled apples in the freezer for at least 8 hours. Remove, and let stand for 20 minutes. Carefully peel apples and cut into quarters. Remove core. Place in a food processor and process until light and fluffy. Remove from food processor and stir through the pulp of the passionfruit.

Serve on a hot summer's night in a well chilled champagne glass. Garnish with segments of fruit, for example, mandarins, oranges, peaches or nectarines.

apple with boysenberry sauce

serves 4

4 apples
½ cup unsweetened apple juice
½ cup water
½ teaspoon mixed spice
⅛ teaspoon ground cloves

1 quantity of vanilla custard (see recipe 'Winter Pears' in this section)
2 cups ripe washed boysenberries

Peel the top half of each apple, leaving stem and leaf (if possible) on. Place in a saucepan with apple juice, water, mixed spice and cloves. Simmer, with lid on until apples are tender. Do not overcook. Remove apples and cool.

Make up custard as per recipe. Remove from heat.

Combine custard and boysenberries and purée in a food processor until smooth. Sauce can be thinned by adding a little milk and puréeing again until smooth. Cool. Refrigerate apples and sauce until serving time. Both apples and sauce should be well chilled.

To serve, place apple on a serving plate and pour sauce around the apple.

banana ice-cream

serves 2
2 bananas

Place unpeeled bananas in the freezer for at least 24 hours. Remove from freezer and carefully cut into 4 pieces (mind your fingers). Carefully cut away the peel and discard. Place bananas in a food processor and process until thick and creamy. Add a dash of vanilla essence if desired. Scoop out and serve with fresh sliced fruit or berries in season.

banquet of berries

serves 10–12

½ large watermelon	1 punnet blackberries
1 punnet strawberries	1 punnet loganberries
1 punnet boysenberries	1 cup dry white wine
1 punnet raspberries	

Using a melon baller, scoop out as many perfect balls as possible, removing seeds until all watermelon flesh is used. Leave some red flesh around the inside of the watermelon, clean away any rough areas and remove all seeds. Rinse the berries and drain. Combine with watermelon balls and fill the watermelon shell.

If all berries are not available to you at the one time, then double up with another variety. Pour over wine and chill thoroughly before serving.

blueberry sauce

400g blueberries
¼ teaspoon zest of lemon
1 tbsp arrowroot mixed with a small amount of pear juice to make a paste

2 teaspoons lemon juice
2 cups natural unsweetened pear juice

Cook blueberries in pear juice with lemon juice and lemon zest. As it slowly comes to the boil, add arrowroot and stir until sauce thickens. If a thicker sauce is desired, add more arrowroot.

Use on wholemeal pancakes, over homemade ice-cream, dessert toppings and especially good with baked apple.

blueberries and sour cream

serves 6

6 cups blueberries
1½ cups low fat ricotta cheese

2 teaspoons vanilla essence
2 tbsps lemon juice

Beat ricotta cheese, vanilla and lemon juice until smooth. Place washed berries on individual serving plates and top with a heaped spoonful of sour cream (approximately ¼ cup per person).

boysenberry apple

serves 1

1 granny smith apple
¼ cup lemon juice
1 cup chilled water

1 cup boysenberries
2 tbsps apple spread (see *Taste of Life*) or puréed cooked apple

Peel the apple. Slice across top of apple to make a flat surface. Using a sharp pointed knife cut a square shape approximately ½ way through the apple. Carefully remove the square. Combine lemon juice and water. Plunge apple into it and leave for 10 minutes. Place in the freezer for 1 hour prior to serving. Purée ½ cup boysenberries and apple spread. Chill.

To serve, place apple case on a dessert plate. Fill with remaining boysenberries and pour over boysenberry sauce.

citrus cantaloup

serves 4

3 cantaloup
2 oranges

2 grapefruit

Using a zig-zag knife (or try cutting a zig-zag pattern, after slicing cantaloup in half) cut 2 cantaloup in half. Remove seeds. Peel the remaining cantaloup, cut in half and remove seeds. Feed portions of the melon into a juicer (if you do not have a juicer use 1 cup of orange juice).

Peel the oranges and grapefruit, making sure to remove all pith. Segment the fruit by cutting on either side of the membrane and remove each segment. Place fruit segments in a bowl. Pour over the cantaloup juice and leave in the refrigerator for at least 1 hour. Chill cantaloup shells also.

To serve, place a cantaloup shell on a serving plate and fill with fruit segments and remaining juice.

fresh blueberries and tofu

Blueberries are relatively a new fruit in the Australian fruit market. They are a convenience food in that they need no peeling, pitting or coring. They are an excellent source of Vitamin A and Vitamin C. They make a delicious jam spread, sauce and muffins, but here they are teamed with Tofu for a light snack or dessert.

Tofu is a soybean curd. It is a protein source, low in fats and entirely free of cholesterol. It is tasty in salads, dressings and sandwiches, but its rather bland flavour teams well with the distinct flavour of the blueberries. Cut it into small cubes for serving.

fresh fruit salad

This looks best on a glass plater, about dinner plate size. Choose fruits in season. On each platter arrange five different fruits very thinly sliced.

Suggestions:

2 large strawberries, thinly sliced
½ kiwi fruit, thinly sliced
slice of pineapple, thinly sliced

wedge of cantaloup, thinly sliced
1 nectarine, stoned and thinly sliced
1 passionfruit

Cut 1 passionfruit in half for each platter. Place passionfruit in the centre of platter and arrange thinly sliced fruit around it. Serve fruits chilled.

Segmenting Fruit:
Oranges, lemons and grapefruits are easily segmented.

Use a sharp knife. Place the fruit upright on a board and pare off the peel and pith in even slices. The segments are cut out individually after the fruit has been peeled and all traces of white pith between the rind and the flesh have been removed carefully.

ginger pears

serves 6

6 pears
1½ cups apple juice
1 × 2cm piece fresh ginger, peeled

2 teaspoons finely grated lemon rind

Peel pears, leaving stems on. Place in a saucepan so they all stand up. Pour over apple juice. Add a piece of ginger and lemon rind. Simmer until pears are soft, but do not overcook them. Remove from heat. Cover and leave to stand until cold.

Place in a serving bowl. Remove ginger. Refrigerate. Serve chilled with small amount of juice.

green goblet

serves 4

1 honey-dew melon
4 kiwi fruit
2 granny smith apples
¼ cup lemon juice
small bunch green grapes

1 cup apple juice
1 cinnamon stick
rind of 1 lemon, cut into very thin strips

Peel the honey-dew melon. Cut in half and remove seeds. Cut each half again. Cut into wafer thin slices, or use a small melon ball scoop to make small balls. Peel kiwi fruit and cut each into 8 slices. Wash the apples. Remove the cores. Leaving skin on, cut apples into julienne strips. (The skin should be visible on the ends.) Place the apple in a bowl and toss in the lemon juice. Wash grapes and remove from stem.

110

Combine apple juice, cinnamon stick and lemon rind in a small saucepan. Simmer for 10 minutes. Remove from heat and leave to cool. Refrigerate to chill.

Arrange fruit in goblets. Pour over an equal quantity of juice and return to refrigerator to chill well.

jellied oranges

serves 4

3 oranges
1 cup unsweetened orange juice
2 tbsps apple juice concentrate

1 tbsp gelatine
¼ cup boiling water

Dissolve gelatine in boiling water and leave to cool. Peel oranges and remove all pith. Cut oranges in half and in half again. Cut into thin slices and place into a small serving bowl. Pour over the combined orange and apple juice concentrate. Stir in the gelatine mixture. Refrigerate.

kiwi fruit ice

serves 2
2 kiwi fruit

Peel the kiwi fruit and cut into four. Place in a plastic container and into the freezer for at least 8 hours. Remove from freezer and let stand for 15 minutes. Place in a food processor and process until thick and creamy.

Use a small melon baller to scoop kiwi ice into small balls and use to serve with fresh fruit. For example, place slices of kiwi fruit and pineapple in a dessert goblet and top with kiwi fruit ice balls.

kiwi fruit jelly

serves 4

4 kiwi fruit
⅔ cup dry wine
¼ cup unsweetened apple juice

1 tbsp gelatine
¼ cup boiling water

Dissolve gelatine in boiling water and leave to cool. Slice kiwi fruit and place in a small serving bowl, pour over the wine and apple juice. Stir in the gelatine mixture. Refrigerate.

orange tang

serves 1

2 oranges   1 tbsp apple juice concentrate

Peel oranges and remove all pith. Cut into quarters and place in the freezer for at least 8 hours. Remove from freezer and let stand for 15 minutes. Place in a food processor with the apple juice concentrate and process until smooth. Spoon into a glass. Top with orange segments and serve on a hot summer's day – delightful!

passionfruit delight

serves 6

300ml non-fat natural yoghurt
½ cup passionfruit pulp
¼ cup unsweetened orange/apple
   juice
1 teaspoon grated lemon rind

½ cup boiling water
1 tbsp gelatine
3 egg whites
6 passionfruit
2 oranges, peeled and segmented

Fold passionfruit pulp through yoghurt. Dissolve gelatine in boiling water, add orange juice and lemon rind. Add to the passionfruit mixture. Beat egg whites until stiff. Fold egg whites through the passionfruit mixture. Pour into individual glass serving dishes or small moulds.

To serve, place glass serving dish on a small plate. Cut the passionfruit in half. Serve alongside the passionfruit delight and garnish with orange segments, or alternatively turn mould out onto a serving dish. Serve with a whole passionfruit which has been cut in half and garnish with orange segments.

strawberries and 'whipped cream'

serves 6

350–400g fresh strawberries
1 cup 'whipped cream' (see recipe
   'Banana Date Steamed
   Pudding' in Special Occasion
   Desserts section)

Wash strawberries. Place in individual dishes and chill. Top with 1 heaped tablespoon of 'whipped cream' per dish.

watermelon bubbles

(an excellent way to start or finish a meal)

serves 4

½ watermelon
rind of 1 orange or grapefruit, cut
  into very fine small strips
1 × 2cm piece of fresh ginger
  peeled

2 cups unsweetened orange juice
1 cup water
¾ cup thinly sliced water chestnuts

Using a melon baller, press down firmly into the watermelon to remove as many perfectly round balls as possible. Remove any seeds. When all the balls have been removed from the top of the melon, slice melon straight across, under the scooped-out portion. Then scoop out more balls until all the watermelon has been used.

Place any left-over flesh, seeds and outer skin removed in a saucepan with the orange rind, ginger, orange juice and water. Bring to the boil. Simmer until liquid is half its original quantity. Remove from heat. Strain, and discard flesh and remaining ginger. Leave to cool. Pour over watermelon balls. Add water chestnuts and chill well.

wine jelly

serves 2

1 cup dry white wine
2 teaspoons gelatine
1 teaspoon lemon juice

sliced fresh fruit (kiwi fruit,
  strawberries, nectarines,
  peaches, grapes, stoned cherries
  etc.)

Combine wine, gelatine and lemon juice in a container and place over a pan of boiling water. Stir until gelatine is dissolved. Set aside to cool.

Place fruit (approximately ½ cup per serving) in the bottom of a tall wine glass. Pour over a small amount of gelatine mixture and leave to set in the refrigerator. When firm, top with remaining gelatine mixture. Refrigerate.

winter pears

serves 6

6 pears

2 cups unsweetened dark grape juice

2 teaspoons finely grated orange rind

2 teaspoons arrowroot

¼ cup water.

Peel pears, leaving stems on. Pour the grape juice into a large saucepan, and stand pears upright in it. Cover and simmer until pears are tender. Remove from heat and leave for 1 hour covered. Remove pears carefully to individual serving bowls. Return juice to stove and slowly bring to the boil. Stir in arrowroot (to which the water has been added and a paste made). Turn off heat. Stir briskly as it thickens. Pour a small amount over each pear. Serve with Vanilla Custard.

Vanilla Custard:

1 cup skim milk

1 tbsp vanilla essence

2 tbsps cornflour

2 tbsps skim milk (extra)

Combine skim milk and vanilla essence in a small saucepan. Make a paste with the extra skim milk and cornflour. Bring skim milk and vanilla to the boil. As bubbles appear, stir in cornflour mixture. Turn heat down and stir for at least 2 minutes. Serve.

special occasion desserts

Every now and then, we break away from our favourite fruit desserts and treat ourselves to a special occasion dessert. Some of the ingredients should be used moderately and I suggest, kept for special treats.

banana date steamed pudding

serves 6–8

1 cup dates
1 cup sultanas
1 teaspoon vanilla essence
2 small mashed bananas
1 cup plain wholemeal flour

1 teaspoon bicarbonate of soda
1 teaspoon baking powder
1 teaspoon cinnamon
1 teaspoon nutmeg
2 egg whites

'Whipped Cream':

1 cup low fat ricotta cheese
¾ cup natural unsweetened fruit

juice, (apple, orange, pear, peach or apricot)
2 teaspoons vanilla essence

Custard:

2 cups skim milk
2 tbsps unsweetened orange juice

1 tbsp vanilla essence
3 tbsps arrowroot

To make pudding:

Place dates and sultanas in a food processor and mince finely. Add vanilla and bananas and mix well.

Sift the dry ingredients. Fold flour through the fruit mixture. Beat egg whites until stiff. Fold through mixture. Pour into a lightly greased pudding basin. Seal.

Place in a saucepan and fill to 3cm from the top of pudding basin with boiling water. Keep just boiling for 1½–1¾ hours. Serve with 'whipped cream' or custard.

115

To make 'whipped cream':
Whip all ingredients until smooth. Chill.

To make custard:
Combine all ingredients and mix well. Bring slowly to the boil in a small saucepan. Stir continuously until the custard thickens.

banana mousse

serves 6

2 frozen bananas
1/4 cup lemon juice
3 cups low fat evaporated milk, well chilled
2 teaspoons vanilla essence

2 tbsps gelatine
1/4 cup boiling water
3 egg whites
1/2–1 teaspoon nutmeg

Peel bananas and purée. Add lemon juice. Beat milk until thick and creamy. Fold through bananas. Add vanilla essence. Mix gelatine with boiling water. Fold through banana mixture. Beat egg whites until stiff. Fold through with nutmeg. Pour into a mould or individual glass goblets.

Serve with 'whipped cream' (see banana date steamed pudding recipe in this section) and slices of fresh banana.

For special occasions add 1 to 2 teaspoons of rum.

banana yoghurt pie

serves 6

Base:

2 cups rolled oats
1 cup dates
1 tbsp vanilla essence

2 tbsps unsweetened orange juice
2 tbsps carob powder

Filling:

2 frozen bananas, peeled and chopped
1 cup low fat evaporated skim milk
1/2 teaspoon vanilla essence

1 cup non-fat yoghurt
1 tbsp gelatine
1/4 cup boiling water

Topping:

1 banana, thinly sliced
1/4 cup lemon juice

1 teaspoon nutmeg

To make base:

Combine base ingredients in a food processor and process until mixture begins to stick together (approximately 3 minutes). Do not over process. Line a 23cm pie dish with foil. Press mixture thinly around sides and base. Press down firmly. Refrigerate.

To make filling:

Pour the boiling water over the gelatine and stir to dissolve. Set aside to cool. Place frozen bananas in a food processor and process until smooth. Add milk. Process for a further 3 to 5 minutes, until thick and creamy and doubled in size. Add vanilla essence, yoghurt and mix well. Add gelatine dissolved in boiling water. Pour over base. Refrigerate until firm (at least 2 to 3 hours).

Garnish the top with thinly sliced bananas (soak in lemon juice first). Sprinkle over nutmeg.

blueberry cheesecake

serves 12

Base:

2 cups wholemeal breadcrumbs	1 egg white
8 almonds in their skins	1 teaspoon almond essence
2 tbsps rolled oats	

Filling:

250g non-fat cottage cheese	1 tbsp gelatine
250g low fat ricotta cheese	1/3 cup boiling water
1/4 cup unsweetened apple juice	1 cup puréed cooked apple, cold
2 tbsps lemon juice	2 egg whites
1 teaspoon vanilla essence	

Topping:

3 tbsps blueberry conserve	1 teaspoon gelatine
1/4 cup unsweetened apple juice	

To make base:

Combine breadcrumbs, almonds and rolled oats in a food processor. Process until almonds are finely ground. Add egg whites and almond essence and process until egg white is absorbed. Press the crumbs onto the base of a lightly greased springform cheese cake tin. Cook at 180°C for 15–20 minutes or until lightly brown. Remove and let stand to cool, while you prepare the filling.

To make filling:
Combine cheeses, apple juice, lemon juice and vanilla essence in the food processor and process until smooth. Dissolve gelatine in boiling water. Let cool slightly and add to cheese mixture. Mix well. Add apples. Beat egg whites until stiff and gently fold through. Pour over the base and refrigerate for 2 hours.

To make topping:
Combine all ingredients and stir over a simmering heat until gelatine has dissolved. Let stand to cool. Pour over cheesecake and return to the refrigerator. Refrigerate for at least 2 hours prior to serving. The flavour will improve as the cheesecake stands.

blueberry yoghurt swirl

serves 1

2 tbsps blueberry jam spread (see recipe in Spreads Section)
2 tbsps water
1 teaspoon arrowroot

¾ cup non-fat yoghurt
½ cup cooked apple purée
¼ cup fresh blueberries

Place blueberry conserve, water and arrowroot in a small saucepan. Stir thoroughly and bring to the boil. When sauce thickens remove from the heat and set aside to cool.

Place ¼ cup yoghurt in a tall thin parfait glass. Mix ½ cup yoghurt with apple purée. Pour over yoghurt. Stir blueberry sauce through the apple and yoghurt.

coffee mousse pie

serves 12

Base:

1 cup wholemeal breadcrumbs
½ cup rolled oats
½ teaspoon cinnamon

½ teaspoon ground ginger
1 tbsp unsweetened apple juice

Filling:

2 cups chilled low fat evaporated skim
   milk
2 tbsps apple juice concentrate
2 teaspoons vanilla essence
½ cup unsweetened orange juice
2 teaspoons decaffeinated coffee (or
   coffee substitute)

2 tbsps gelatine
¼ cup boiling water
3 teaspoons finely grated orange rind
3 egg whites

Topping:

mandarin segments

To make base:

Combine base ingredients in a food processor. Process until combined.
Press into a foil lined cheese cake springform tin. Cook at 180°C for 15
minutes until lightly browned. Remove from oven and leave to cool.

To make filling:

Beat evaporated milk until thick and creamy. Add apple juice concentrate, vanilla essence, orange juice and coffee. Beat lightly until
combined. Mix gelatine in boiling water until dissolved. Mix through milk
mixture. Beat egg whites until stiff. Fold through milk mixture with
orange rind. Pour over base. Refrigerate for 2 hours.

Decorate the top with mandarin segments.

frozen fruit salad

serves 6–8

2 teaspoons gelatine
2 tbsps boiling water
2 tbsps skim milk powder
1 × 375ml can low fat evaporated
   skim milk (well chilled)
2 tbsps apple juice concentrate
2 bananas, thinly sliced
3 passionfruit (pulp)

2 apricots, finely chopped
2 peaches or nectarines, finely
   chopped
1 cup sliced strawberries
½ cantaloup (peeled and seeds
   removed), finely chopped
2 teaspoons vanilla essence

Dissolve gelatine in boiling water. Beat together the powdered milk,
evaporated milk and apple juice concentrate. Beat in gelatine. Place in
chilled freezer trays and freeze until just mushy. Pour into a chilled bowl
and beat until smooth and doubled in volume. Fold through fruits and
vanilla. Pour into a mould or a basin lined with foil. Freeze overnight.

Before serving, remove from freezer and let soften slightly.

119

frozen melon yoghurt

serves 4

1 ripe honey-dew melon
1 tbsp lemon juice
1 tbsp gelatine
2 tbsps boiling water

1 tbsp apple juice concentrate
450g non-fat yoghurt
½ cup preserved ginger, finely
  chopped

Peel honey-dew melon and purée flesh until just mushy (not liquid). Stir in lemon juice. Dissolve gelatine in boiling water and stir through. Pour into a chilled freezer tray and freeze until mushy.

Remove from freezer and tip into a chilled bowl. Beat until smooth. Wash ginger to remove excess sugar and pat dry. Fold ginger through melon yoghurt mixture and return to freezer.

Serve partly frozen with slices of kiwi fruit or mandarin segments.

pineapple yoghurt pie

serves 8

Base:

1 cup dried fruit medley
1½ cups rolled oats
½ cup almonds in their skins

1 teaspoon vanilla essence
¼ cup unsweetened orange juice

Filling:

1 tbsp gelatine
¼ cup boiling water
1 cup finely chopped fresh or
  bottled pineapple

¼ cup pineapple juice
1 teaspoon grated lemon juice
⅓ cup apple juice concentrate
2 cups non-fat yoghurt

Topping:

thinly sliced fresh pineapple or kiwi fruit

To make base:

Combine ingredients and process until mixture begins to stick together (approximately 3 to 5 minutes). Do not over process. Line a 23cm pie dish with foil. Press mixture thinly around sides and base. Press down firmly. Refrigerate.

To make filling:
Pour the boiling water over the gelatine and stir to dissolve. Combine pineapple, pineapple juice, lemon rind and apple juice concentrate in a food processor and lightly process to just combine. Add yoghurt and mix well. Add gelatine. Pour over base. Refrigerate until firm (at least 2 to 3 hours).

Garnish the top with thinly sliced pineapple or kiwi fruit.

pumpkin dessert pie

serves 8–10

Base:

½ cup almonds in their skins
¼ cup raisins
1 cup wheat flakes or rolled oats

1½ teaspoons cinnamon
1 tbsp apple juice

Filling:

500g cooked pumpkin
2 tbsps apple juice concentrate
2 teaspoons finely grated orange rind
½ cup soy milk

1 tbsp vanilla
½ cup currants or finely chopped dried apricots
4 egg whites

To make base:
Combine all base ingredients in a food processor and process until it just begins to stick together. Line a 23cm pie dish with foil and press crumb mixture very thinly over base and sides.

To make filling:
Place pumpkin, apple juice concentrate, orange rind, soy milk and vanilla in a food processor and process until smooth. Fold through currants. Beat egg whites until quite stiff and fold through. Pour into base and cook at 180°C for 50 minutes. Serve chilled topped with whipped cream and a shake of nutmeg.

strawberry carob cheesecake

serves 12

Base:

1 cup rolled oats
1 cup almonds in their skins

½ teaspoon nutmeg
1 teaspoon cinnamon

Filling:

500g low fat ricotta cheese
20 dried apricots
½ cup boiling water
2 tbsps carob powder (sifted)
1 teaspoon vanilla essence

1 cup non-fat yoghurt
1 tbsp gelatine
¼ cup boiling water
2 tbsps lemon juice
2 egg whites

Topping:

2 punnets strawberries, sliced.

To make base:

Combine the base ingredients in a food processor and process for 5 minutes. Press crumb mixture into a lightly greased springform cheese cake tin. Press down firmly.

To make filling:

Beat cheese until smooth. Simmer apricots in boiling water for 10 minutes. Purée and cool. Add to the cheese mixture along with carob, vanilla and non-fat yoghurt.

Combine gelatine, boiling water and lemon juice. Stir to dissolve gelatine, and mix into cheese mixture. Beat egg whites until stiff and fold through. Pour over the base and refrigerate for 20 minutes.

Remove and top with finely sliced strawberries. Return to the refrigerator for at least 2 hours prior to serving.

cakes and slices

I can't imagine a dietary lifestyle that doesn't include cakes, slices, scones and biscuits, so I include these following recipes which have become our favourites. Sesame seeds, almonds, sunflower seeds, cold compressed almond oil, natural maple syrup, and walnuts in their shells, are unrefined products, however they are not used on the Nathan Pritikin Maintenance Diet. Except for Special Occasion Almond Apricot Biscuits (Ted's Apricot Fancies), these ingredients have been used as a flavouring ingredient. Unless you sit down and eat a whole cake or all the slice at one sitting (heaven forbid – although they taste good enough to do it!), you will be eating a small amount.

apple and cinnamon yoghurt slice

makes 16 slices

Base:

1 cup wholemeal breadcrumbs
1 cup rolled oats
1 teaspoon cinnamon
1 tbsp unsweetened orange juice
1 egg white

Filling:

200g cottage cheese
400g cooked apple chunks
1 teaspoon vanilla essence
1 teaspoon cinnamon
1 teaspoon nutmeg
½ cup non-fat yoghurt
1 cup sultanas
¼ cup wholemeal plain flour
2 teaspoons finely grated lemon rind
2 egg whites

To make base:

Place breadcrumbs, rolled oats, cinnamon and orange juice in a food processor. Using the blade and the stop start push button, process until breadcrumbs begin to stick together. Add egg white. Process lightly until egg white is absorbed by the breadcrumbs. Do not over process.

Spread breadcrumbs evenly over a foil lined 30cm × 20cm slice tin. Press down firmly. Cook at 150°C for 10 minutes. Remove from oven. Turn oven up to 180°C.

To make filling:
Press cottage cheese through a fine sieve. Add all other ingredients except egg whites and mix well. Beat egg whites until stiff. Gently fold through apple mixture. Pour over base and spread out evenly. Bake at 180°C for 45 minutes. Leave to cool in tin, and cut into slices before removing from tin. Store in refrigerator after two days.

Variation:
Apricot Yoghurt Slice

Substitute cooked chopped apricots for apples. Omit vanilla essence. Use 1 teaspoon of cinnamon and 1 teaspoon of mixed spice.

apricot and bran muffins

makes 24

1 cup cooked apricots, drained
2½ cups plain wholemeal flour, sifted
½ cup bran
1 tbsp baking powder

¾ cup non-fat yoghurt
2 teaspoons vanilla essence
¼ cup orange juice
4 egg whites

Purée apricots in a food processor. Combine dry ingredients and sift. Add to the food processor and blend just a little. Add yoghurt and vanilla. Blend to incorporate. Add orange juice.

Beat egg whites until stiff. Add mixture to egg whites and fold through. Place spoonfuls in lightly oiled muffin tins.

Bake at 220°C for 25 minutes. Serve hot from the oven with apricot fruit spread (see recipe *Taste of Life*). These are much tastier eaten hot rather than cold.

apricot oat slice

makes approximately 24

1 cup dried apricots, finely chopped
1 cup raisins, finely minced
1 cup garbanzo nuts (roasted chick peas, available at health food shops)
1 tbsp sesame seeds (toasted)
½ cup skim milk powder
2 cups rolled oats
2 teaspoons vanilla essence
½ cup unsweetened orange juice

I found the easiest way to combine these ingredients was in the mixer using the dough hook blade. A large food processor or your hands will do the job with a little more effort.

Combine all ingredients and mix together. Press into a foil lined slice tin.

Refrigerate for at least 4 hours. Keep in the refrigerator.

banana and sultana yeast cake

(well worth the effort)

½ cup sultanas
1 teaspoon lemon rind, finely grated
1 tbsp unsweetened orange juice
½ cup ripe banana, mashed
½ cup skim milk
¼ cup non-fat yoghurt
1 teaspoon vanilla essence
1½ teaspoons dry yeast or 15g fresh yeast
¼ cup lukewarm water
4 egg whites
2 cups wholemeal plain flour
2 tbsps fine wholemeal breadcrumbs

Soak sultanas and lemon rind in orange juice. Set aside. Combine mashed banana, milk and yoghurt and mix well. Add vanilla. Combine yeast with water. Stand for 10 minutes in a warm spot. Beat egg whites lightly. Add to yeast. Add flour and lightly stir through. Mix in banana and yoghurt mixture. Set aside in a warm spot to double in size (approximately 1½ hours). Punch down. Add sultana mixture and mix well.

Lightly grease a 6½ cup cake mould and sprinkle over with the breadcrumbs. Shake off the excess. Turn mixture into the cake tin and set aside in a warm place to double in size (approximately 1 hour).

Cook at 180°C for 45 minutes covered with foil. Leave foil on for 10 minutes after removing from oven or remove foil and wrap cake in a tea towel.

Variations:
There are several variations to this cake. Substitute sultanas with other fruits, for example, dates, dried apricots or currants; *or* substitute banana with cooked apple, cooked mashed pumpkin, cooked puréed apricots.

blueberry muffins

makes 18

These are deliciously moist muffins that are best eaten warm, without the need to add any spreads.

2 cups wholemeal plain flour
200g fresh blueberries
½ cup apple juice concentrate
2 teaspoons vanilla essence

2 teaspoons baking powder
¼ cup cold compressed oil
¼ cup non-fat yoghurt
2 egg whites

Sift the flour and baking powder twice. Add blueberries and coat well with the flour. Mix together the oil, apple juice concentrate, yoghurt and vanilla. Make a well in the centre of the flour, and pour in half the mixture. Gently combine without squashing the blueberries. Add remaining mixture. Beat egg whites until stiff. Gently fold through the blueberry mixture until just combined. Spoon into a lightly oiled muffin tray. Cook at 180°C for 25–30 minutes. Remove from oven and cool slightly.

carob hedgehog slice

makes 36

1 cup dates
1 cup sultanas
½ cup almonds in their skins
2 cups rolled oats

1 tbsp vanilla essence
2 tbsps carob powder
    (unsweetened)

Combine all ingredients in a food processor. Process until the mixture begins to stick together. Press into a foil lined 20cm × 30cm slice tin. Refrigerate.

carrot and raisin cake

2½ cups wholemeal plain flour
2 teaspoons baking powder
1 teaspoon baking soda
1 teaspoon cinnamon
½ teaspoon nutmeg
6 walnuts in their shells
¼ cup cold compressed almond oil

1 tbsp apple juice concentrate
⅓ cup non-fat yoghurt
2 teaspoons vanilla essence
2 cups raw carrot, finely minced
½ cup raisins, finely chopped
4 egg whites

Sift the dry ingredients twice. Shell the walnuts, chop roughly and mix in. Combine oil, apple juice concentrate, yoghurt and vanilla essence, mix well. Add carrot and raisins. Mix again. Beat egg whites until stiff. Gently fold them through the fairly stiff carrot mixture. Turn mixture into a foil lined, deep sided 20cm square tin.

Cook at 180°C for 1 hour. Cover with foil for 10 minutes. Remove foil and leave in tin to cool.

cinnamon and oatmeal muffins

makes approximately 16

¾ cup plain flour
2 teaspoons baking powder
2 teaspoons cinnamon
1½ cups rolled oats
4 egg whites
½ cup evaporated milk – low fat

½ cup non-fat yoghurt
1 tbsp apple juice concentrate
2 teaspoons orange rind, finely grated
1 teaspoon vanilla essence
1 cup apple, freshly grated

Sift flour, baking powder and cinnamon. Add rolled oats and mix through. Beat egg whites, add milk, apple juice concentrate, orange rind and vanilla essence. Mix well. Add to flour and fold through. Add grated apple and mix well. Lightly grease muffin tins and sprinkle with bran. Shake off excess. Spoon mixture into muffin tins.

Cook at 190°C for 25 to 30 minutes.

griddle scones

makes 8

2 cups wholemeal flour
1 teaspoon baking soda
1 teaspoon baking powder
1 heaped teaspoon skim milk
    powder
¼ teaspoon cayenne pepper or
    curry powder

¼ cup green capsicum, chopped
2 tbsps low fat grating cheese, finely
    grated
¼ cup celery, chopped
2 tbsps non-fat yoghurt
1 egg white
¼ cup skim milk (approximately)

Sift flour, soda, baking powder, skim milk and cayenne pepper. Add green capsicum, cheese, and celery. Mix in well to coat evenly with flour. Add yoghurt and mix well with fingers. Mix in egg white. Slowly add milk until you have a soft dough (not too sticky). Knead lightly on a floured bench. Flatten down with the palm of your hand to a 1cm thick round shape. Cut into four and cut each corner into 3. Place on a non-stick griddle pan. Cook for 5 minutes on one side and 3 minutes on the other.

To serve, open while hot, add shredded lettuce or sprouts and a slice of tomato. Great for morning tea snack or serve hot at your barbecue. These are best served hot, rather than cold.

lemon munchies

makes approximately 30

1 cup wholemeal plain flour
1 teaspoon cinnamon or mixed
    spice
1 cup rolled oats
½ cup bran
½ cup roasted chick peas, crushed
    slightly

1 apple, peeled and finely chopped
125g dates, finely chopped
4 teaspoons lemon rind, grated
125g low fat ricotta cheese
1 tbsp yoghurt
1 teaspoon baking soda
2 tbsps boiling water

Combine flour, spice, rolled oats, bran and chick peas. Add chopped apple, dates and grated lemon rind. Stir in ricotta cheese and yoghurt. Add soda to boiling water and dissolve. Stir into mixture and mix thoroughly. Roll into small balls. Place on a lightly greased oven tray. Press down lightly with a fork.

Cook for 20 minutes at 180°C.

lemon zucchini muffins

makes approximately 16

2 cups plain flour
1 tbsp baking powder
2 teaspoons lemon rind
½ teaspoon nutmeg
½ cup bran

½ cup currants
4 egg whites
½ cup skim milk
⅓ cup low fat yoghurt
1 cup raw zucchini, grated

Combine flour and baking powder. Sift twice. Add lemon rind, nutmeg and bran. Mix well. Stir in currants. Beat egg whites until stiff. Add milk, yoghurt and zucchini. Pour into flour mixture and gently fold through. Lightly grease muffin tins and sprinkle with wholemeal plain flour or bran. Shake off excess. Spoon mixture into the muffin tins.

Cook at 190°C for 25 minutes.

prune bars

makes approximately 24

⅔ cup finely chopped prunes
⅓ cup finely chopped dried apple
1 tbsp sunflower seeds
1 tbsp sesame seeds (toasted)
½ cup rolled wheat flakes
½ cup raw bran

1 cup rolled oats
½ cup skim milk powder
1 tbsp vanilla essence
⅓ cup unsweetened orange juice
2 teaspoons finely grated lemon rind

Combine the first 8 ingredients in a food processor. Turn on. Quickly add vanilla and orange juice to bind, then lemon rind. Line a 30cm × 20cm slice tin with foil and press mixture into it.

Refrigerate for at least 4 hours. Cut into bars. Keep in an airtight container.

special occasion almond apricot biscuits (ted's apricot fancies)

makes 24

250g almonds in their skins
    (preferably just shelled prior to
    making biscuits)
20 dried apricots or 100g dried apple
1 teaspoon vanilla essence

1 teaspoon apple juice concentrate
1 teaspoon cider vinegar (for a chewy
    texture)
2 egg whites
¼ cup wholemeal plain flour

Combine whole almonds and apricots in a food processor, using the blade, and process for 3 minutes. Add vanilla, apple juice concentrate and vinegar. Beat egg whites until stiff. Fold through almond mixture. Roll into small balls. Roll in wholemeal plain flour. Place on a lightly greased non-stick baking tray. Press down flat.

Cook at 200°C for 10 minutes. Biscuits should be lightly browned around the edges. Do not overcook. Cool on a wire rack and keep in an airtight container.

wholemeal banana date scones

makes approximately 20

2 cups wholemeal plain flour
2 teaspoons baking powder
1 teaspoon baking soda
¼ teaspoon cinnamon
¼ teaspoon mixed spice

1 cup dates (finely chopped)
1 teaspoon finely grated lemon rind
1 small mashed banana
¾ cup skim milk
1 teaspoon lemon juice

Sift flour, baking powder, soda and spices. Add dates, lemon rind, and mix through. Add banana to milk and lemon juice, and add to the flour and date mixture. Mix together and knead lightly. Cut into desired shapes and place on a scone tray. Cook at 250°C, 15 to 20 minutes.

Eat while warm or freeze to keep. If frozen, wrap in foil and place in a hot oven to thaw.

zucchini and currant cake

2½ cups wholemeal plain flour
2 teaspoons baking powder
1 teaspoon baking soda
1 teaspoon cinnamon
1 teaspoon mixed spice
¼ cup cold compressed almond oil

½ cup non-fat yoghurt
1 tbsp natural maple syrup
2 cups raw zucchini, grated
1 cup currants
4 egg whites

Sift the dry ingredients twice. Combine oil, yoghurt, maple syrup and mix well. Add zucchini and currants. Mix again. Fold in flour. Beat egg whites until stiff peaks form. Gently fold them through the fairly stiff zucchini mixture. Turn it into a foil lined, deep sided 20cm square tin.

Cook at 180°C for 1 hour. Cover with foil for 10 minutes. Remove foil and leave in tin to cool.

home preserves

Recently I discovered the art of preserving my own fruits and vegetables in bottles without the need to add any sugar or salt. It is effortless, the results are great and it enables us to enjoy the natural goodness and flavour of fruit and vegetables long after their season has ended.

The compliments I receive about 'my shelves of many colours' are rewards enough, but the real bonus is that we can enjoy the fruits and vegetables in season at their peak in quality and usually at the right price, all year round, ready to use without the need for a lot of extra fuss.

As a family we have enjoyed the subtle flavours of the various combinations of fruits and vegetables and occasionally a dash of spice or vinegar.

I especially delight in the fact that there are no added sugars or salts or preservatives and colours – the true flavour is the real flavour.

If you do not have a preserving unit, I would like to encourage you to save your extra cents and invest in one. The latest model is inexpensive. It is simply filled with water, switched on and allowed to cook for the required amount of time – usually about 1 hour. Bottles are then removed from the unit, cooled and stored to be enjoyed as you require them.

In recipes calling for cooked fruits, use bottled fruit. Drain the vegetables and use in salads or other suitable recipes.

Note:
All recipes require preserving bottles or jars. For quantities, other bottle sizes and processing details refer to an updated book on fruit and vegetable preserving techniques. I would recommend Australian Preserving with Fowlers Vacola *by Margaret Hill.*

131

apples

Served as a cooked fruit:

Cut apples into quarters (peel removed if desired). Pack into bottles. Pour in 2 tablespoons of lemon juice or ¼ cup unsweetened orange juice or ¼ cup unsweetened pear juice and top up with water.

For an interesting flavour, add 1 cinnamon stick down the side of the bottle before sealing.

Process using usual method.

Suggested use: serve with porridge, muesli or yoghurt.

Served in desserts, strudels, spread, cakes and muffins:

Peel apples and remove seeds. Work quickly to avoid discolouration. Roughly chop the apples and fill bottles. Add 1 to 2 tablespoons of lemon juice and top up with water and/or some whole cloves.

Combine with another fruit for added interest, for example, rhubarb, roughly chopped. Add ½ cup unsweetened grape juice then top up with water or ½ cup unsweetened orange juice then top up with water.

Process using usual method.

Suggested use: Apple Banana Fruit Strudel, Apple and Cinnamon Muffins.

apricots

Served as a cooked fruit:

I like to preserve apricots in their whole state, although it is a little more difficult in the packing. However the stone of the apricot tends to add an almond-like flavour after bottles stand on the shelf for a period of time.

The apricots simply need to be washed and stalks removed, then packed in bottles very tightly. Pour in ¼ cup to ½ cup unsweetened orange juice and top up with water, *or* cook some apricots in 1 litre of water until quite soft. Remove stones. Push through a sieve. Pour this liquid over apricots.

For special occasions a dash of brandy could also be added.

Process in the usual method.

Suggested use: serve in dessert goblets.

banquet of berries; citrus cantaloup

winter pears

banana ice-cream; orange tang; kiwi fruit ice

preserves: pineapple, bananas

pears, apricots, tomatoes, mixed pickled vegetables,
peaches, blueberries

wholemeal banana date scones; special occasion almond apricot biscuits;
lemon munchies

blueberry muffins with blueberry jam spread and 'whipped cream'

Christmas dinner: chicken terrine with baked herb tomatoes and baked potatoes; Christmas pudding; Christmas cake

bananas

Served as a cooked fruit:
This is rather a different – but certainly a tasty way – to eat your bananas.

Peel and slice as you like. Pack tightly in bottles. Add 2 tablespoons of lemon juice and top with water, unsweetened orange juice, unsweetened pineapple juice or unsweetened grape juice.

Suggested use: serve with porridge, muesli or yoghurt.

Served in desserts:
Add the pulp of 3 large passionfruit after the 2 tablespoons of lemon juice. Top with water. *Or* create a layer effect in the bottle with slices of banana, then strips of dried apricot (repeat). Top up with unsweetened orange juice after adding 2 tablespoons of lemon juice.

Process in the usual method.

Suggested use: top with yoghurt or a light warm custard.

beetroot

Wash beetroot thoroughly, careful not to break the skin. Place in a saucepan with enough water to cover. Bring to the boil and simmer for 1 hour to 2 hours or until beetroot skin comes away easily. Remove from heat. Run under cold water to remove skins. Cut as desired or leave whole (if small enough). Pack tightly into bottles. Top up bottles with half water, half cider vinegar, or half unsweetened orange juice and half cider vinegar.

Process in the usual method.

Suggested uses: use in salads and sandwiches.

Bitey Beetroot:
Wash beetroot thoroughly. Peel and cut into ½cm chips. Pack into bottles tightly. Top up with cider vinegar or half water and half cider vinegar.

Process in the usual method.

Suggested uses: use in salads. Use as a vegetable in platter of vegetables.

citrus fruits salad
grapefruit

Peel and cut away the pith of the citrus fruit. Cut into segments, removing membrane, and pips. Mandarins need not have membrane removed, but should have pips removed to avoid a bitter taste. Pack tightly into bottles and top up with water, half water and half unsweetened orange juice, unsweetened orange juice, *or* unsweetened pineapple juice.

Process using usual method.

Suggested use: use as the base for a fruit salad taste you'll find very different and delicious, *or* serve chilled as a first course on a hot summer's night.

mandarins

As above.

oranges

As above.

fruit salad

pineapple, peaches, apricots, pears, mandarins, oranges, grapefruit, cherries (stoned), grapes (green and purple), passionfruit, kiwi fruit, nectarines, plums.

Select your own combination. Clean fruit and cut into even sizes or leave whole (for example, grapes/cherries). Pack tightly into bottles and top up with unsweetened apple, orange or pineapple juice.

Process using usual method.

Suggested use: serve chilled as a fruit salad dessert. For a special occasion add 2 teaspoons brandy.

freshly picked mixed vegetables

Vegetables: *carrots, radishes, turnips, cucumber, capsicums (red and green). celery, pumpkin (butternut), green beans, snow peas, zucchini.*

Wash all vegetables and peel if necessary. Cut into strips, 2cm cubes, or slice diagonally. Pack into bottles tightly. Top up with ⅔ cider vinegar and ⅓ water.

Process in the usual method.

Suggested uses: serve to nibble at for special occasions. Use in salads.

peaches

Remove the peel, leave whole, halve or cut each half into 4 slices. Pack tightly into bottles.

I like to add a few whole almonds and some thin strips of orange peel (pith removed) or 2 teaspoons of finely grated lemon rind to each bottle before topping up with water or half water and half unsweetened orange juice. You might also like to add a whole nutmeg or cinnamon stick to each bottle.

Process using usual method.

Suggested use: Peach Passionfruit Cheesecake (see 'Apricot and Passionfruit Cheesecake' in Christmas Dinner section).

pears

Pears can be preserved whole, halved or quartered. Remove skin, seeds and stalk (stalk can be left on if preserving the pear in its whole state). Pack tightly into bottles. Top up with water and add a few mint leaves or top up with half water and half unsweetened dark grape juice.

Or cook some pears in unsweetened orange juice until pears are quite soft. Strain and use this liquid to top up bottles. Add the pulp of 6 passionfruit to each bottle and top up with water.

Process in the usual method.

Suggested use: Mint Pears as a first course. Winter Pears.

pineapple

Remove top and bottom of pineapple. Cut into slices, then peel and core pineapple. Leave in chunky circles, or cut into small chunks or just roughly chop the flesh. Juice one whole pineapple (ends and peel removed). Add an equal quantity of water to the quantity of pineapple juice. Pack pineapple firmly into bottles and top up with the diluted pineapple juice.

Process using the usual method.

Suggested use: use in fruit salads, vegetable salads, excellent with steamed chicken *or* in sweet and sour. Best eaten just as it is.

strawberries

If you are lucky enough to have your own strawberry patch, it is worthwhile preserving this fruit to use when not in season for sauces and spreads. During the processing, they tend to shrink and lose some of their bright colour which detracts from their appearance and use in many other dishes.

Gently wash fruit and drain. Place strawberries in a saucepan. Cover with half water and half unsweetened orange juice. Slowly bring to the boil. When it reaches boiling temperature remove from heat, cover and let stand for 4 hours. Strain and reserve liquid. Place strawberries in bottles.

Return liquid to saucepan and bring to the boil. Boil until reduced to half. Leave to cool slightly. Pour over strawberries.

Process in the usual method.

Suggested uses: thicken with arrowroot to make a sauce. Use sauce in pancakes or on top of cheesecake. Add fruit pectin to make a strawberry spread. Fold through equal quantity of apple purée and chill, for a summer breakfast treat.

tomatoes

Tomatoes are such a versatile fruit; and although availablenearly all year around they are at their best at the beginning of the year. Preserving them retains them at their best. They can be preserved peeled or unpeeled, whole, halved or roughly chopped. Pack them firmly into bottles so there is no need to add any liquid except 1 tablespoon of lemon juice.

Process in the usual method.

Suggested uses: purée for a quick tomato juice. Base for a tomato soup. Add to casseroles. Add to sauces, for example, spaghetti.

tomato and leeks

Peel tomatoes and chop roughly. Use only the white part of the leek and wash thoroughly. Slice leeks very thinly. Combine equal quantities of tomato and leeks and mix well before packing tightly into bottles. Top up with 1 tablespoon of lemon juice, 2 tablespoons of cider vinegar and water.

Process in the usual method.

Suggested uses: add to casseroles. Add to soups. Base for a soup. Thicken and use on a pizza base. Thicken and use cold in sandwiches or salads.

tomato and zucchini

Peel tomatoes and chop roughly. Remove ends of zucchini, wash and slice thinly. Pack tightly into bottles using equal quantities of tomato and zucchini. Top up with 1 tablespoon of lemon juice, 2 tablespoons of cider vinegar and water.

Process in the usual method.

Suggested uses: add to casseroles. Thicken with cornflour to make a sauce. Thicken with cornflour, place in a casserole dish, top with breadcrumbs and finely grated low fat grating cheese. Serve as an accompaniment to a main meal.

137

breakfast time

Breakfast time is the start of a new day and you'll need plenty of energy to make it a worthwhile day so make it a worthwhile breakfast. It need not become a monotonous routine of coffee, orange juice and toast. Let your imagination run wild with the recipes in this section. I suggest you nibble at a piece of fresh fruit while you make your decision.

apple and banana sandwich

serves 1

1 large granny smith apple
1 banana
2 tbsps sultanas

½ teaspoon cinnamon
½ teaspoon mixed spice

Core apple. Cut apple into 4 equal rounds. Mash banana with sultanas, cinnamon and mixed spice. Spread banana mixture on to the top side of the bottom piece of the apple. Place next slice of apple on top and repeat with banana filling until all filling and apple slices are used. Wrap in foil. Place in small casserole dish. Add water to come up a few centimetres from the bottom and cook in a hot oven for 20 minutes.

baked banana boat

serves 1

1 large banana
2 dates, finely chopped
2 tbsps apple, cooked
cinnamon

1 tbsp lemon or orange juice
2 tbsps non-fat natural yoghurt
2 tbsps sugar-free toasted muesli

139

Make a slit from top to bottom of banana in the skin only. Using fingers gently ease away the skin from the banana, still leaving the banana in the skin. Make another slit down the banana from top to bottom but do not cut banana completely in half. Gently ease the banana open and spoon in dates. Spread evenly along the banana. Top with the apple and spread over evenly. Sprinkle with cinnamon. Pour juice over the apple filling. Wrap in foil loosely and secure. Bake in a hot oven for 15 minutes.

To serve, place banana still in its skin in a bowl. Spoon over yoghurt and sprinkle top with muesli.

banana boy

serves 1

1 banana	½–¾ cup sugar-free toasted
1 egg white	muesli
dash of orange juice	1 tbsp non-fat natural yoghurt

Peel banana. Beat egg white and orange juice with a fork. Roll banana in egg white and then roll in muesli. Press muesli firmly onto banana using your hand. Cook in a hot oven for 10 minutes or until banana is soft.

To serve, place banana in a bowl. Add yoghurt and sprinkle with cinnamon, mixed spice or nutmeg.

breakfast juices

serves 1

Apart from freshly squeezed orange juice you might like to try some of these combinations.

Banana Milkshake: 1 small ripe banana, ½ cup skim milk, ½ teaspoon vanilla essence, dash of nutmeg (optional), 4 ice blocks.

Chop banana roughly. Place all ingredients in a blender. Blend until smooth and frothy.

Carrot and Apple: use baby carrots for their sweetness. You need 4–6 carrots and 2 granny smith apples.

Wash carrots and peel and core apples. Juice the remaining fruit. Pour into long thin glasses. Add ice blocks and garnish with slice of cucumber, lemon and a sprig of mint.

Celery and Pineapple: 2 cups fresh chopped pineapple, 2 stalks celery (from inside of celery bunch).

Juice and pour into glass. Add crushed ice.

Grapefruit and Orange: 2 oranges, 1 grapefruit.

Peel and remove pith. Juice the remaining flesh. Pour into a chilled glass. Garnish with a slice of orange.

Pineapple, Mango and Passionfruit: 1 cup fresh chopped pineapple, 1 cup mango flesh, ¼ cup passionfruit pulp.

Juice the pineapple and mango and stir through passionfruit pulp.

Tomato Spicer: 2 cups tomato juice, 1 cup low fat yoghurt, pinch of garlic, 1 teaspoon finely grated lemon rind, 2 teaspoons finely chopped red capsicum, strips of red capsicum and green capsicum to garnish.

Process until smooth. Chill well. Serve in long thin glasses, and garnish with capsicum strips.

Note: this recipe serves 3.

N.B. In all recipes using skim milk or non-fat yoghurt, you could also substitute soymilk.

cantaloup shell

serves 1

½ cantaloup	1 banana
2 tbsps low fat ricotta cheese	juice of 1 lemon
¼ teaspoon vanilla essence	

Remove seeds from cantaloup and make a neat cavity. Combine ricotta cheese and vanilla essence and mix well. Line the cavity of the cantaloup with ricotta cheese and fill with slices of banana. Pour over the juice of the lemon to completely cover banana.

Cover with foil and refrigerate for 10 minutes. Serve cold.

citrus segments

serves 1

½ orange	2 teaspoons finely grated lemon rind
½ grapefruit	mint leaves to garnish
juice of 1 orange	

Using a sharp knife, pare off the peel and pith from orange and grapefruit. To cut segments, cut on either side of the membrane and remove segments. Arrange segments on a plate. Place juice and rind in a small saucepan and heat, but do not boil. Stir lemon rind through juice while heating. Remove from heat. Let cool, but not necessarily to get cold. Pour juice over fruit segments, garnish with mint leaves and serve.

For special occasion serve in a grapefruit shell or orange shell.

fish grill

serves 1

1 fillet of fish	2 tbsps spring onions, chopped
water	slices of tomato
lemon juice	fresh basil, finely chopped
2 tbsps low fat ricotta cheese	

Lightly poach fillet of fish in a non-stick pan with water and lemon juice. Carefully remove from pan and place on a sheet of foil. Spread fish with ricotta cheese and sprinkle over chopped spring onions. Top with slices of tomato and finely chopped fresh basil. Place under griller until nicely browned.

fruit platter

serves 1

There is no better way to start the day than the flavours of fresh fruits. Choose 4 different varieties of fruit, depending on what is in season. Take just a little time to arrange them artistically on the platter and always serve the fruit chilled.

Some Selections:

2 pineapple circles	4 kiwi fruit quarters
8 strawberries	1 whole pear
1 peach	1 nectarine
8 strawberries	1 banana
1 fig	1 small bunch of green grapes
1 banana	1 apple
12 cherries	1 plum
2 apricots	1 apple

1 fig
kiwi fruit slices

bunch of purple grapes
mandarin segments

slices of papaw
berries of choice

slices of honey-dew melon
cantaloup balls

fruity french toast

serves 4

4 slices thickly sliced wholemeal
  bread
½ cup skim milk
1 teaspoon vanilla
2 egg whites

⅛ teaspoon cinnamon
2 bananas, mashed
1 orange, peeled and thinly sliced
2 granny smith apples, grated

Combine milk, vanilla, egg whites and cinnamon. Beat with a fork until thoroughly mixed. Dip slices of bread into milk mixture, coating each side. Place on a non-stick griddle and cook for 2 to 3 minutes on either side or until well browned. Divide mashed banana equally between the 4 slices of French toast, and spread over while toast is still hot. Top with thin slices of orange and grated apple. Eat immediately.

mushroom and tomato rolls

serves 4

4 wholemeal bread rolls, remove tops
  and hollow out the centre
300g mushrooms, peeled
½ cup water
4 cooked tomatoes and juice
  (approximately ¼ cup)

2 tbsps chopped parsley
2 tbsps chopped chives or ¼ cup
  chopped shallots
pinch of nutmeg (optional)
¼ cup water
2 tbsps cornflour

Cook mushrooms in ½ cup water over a gentle heat for 1 hour. Add tomatoes and juice, parsley and chives. Cook for a further 5 minutes. Add nutmeg. Mix cornflour and water and stir through mushrooms to thicken.

Place rolls under griller until well browned top and bottom. Place each roll on individual serving plates and spoon mushrooms and tomato mixture into each roll. Serve.

oat porridge

serves 1

½ cup rolled oats
1 cup water

1 teaspoon vanilla essence

Combine all ingredients in a small saucepan. Slowly bring to the boil. Simmer for 3 minutes, stirring continuously. Pour into a bowl. Serve with home preserved fruits, and a small amount of the fruit juice.

puffed millet and apple

serves 1

¾ cup puffed millet
½ cup apple, cooked

dash of cinnamon
½ cup skim milk

Place millet in breakfast bowl. Top with apple, dash of cinnamon and pour over milk.

rice with fruit

serves 1

¾ cup wholemeal brown rice, cooked and warm
1 banana
½ cup apple, cooked

½ cup skim milk
dash of nutmeg
2 tbsps non-fat yoghurt (optional)

Place warm rice in a breakfast bowl. Peel banana and chop up. Place in a blender with apple and whip until smooth. Spoon on top of rice. Pour over milk. Add a good dash of nutmeg to flavour and top with yoghurt (optional).

shredded wheats, strawberries and 'cream'

serves 1

4 shredded wheats
1 cup strawberries, hulled
2–3 tbsps 'whipped cream'

(see recipe 'Banana Date Steamed Pudding' in Special Occasion Desserts section)

Place shredded wheats in breakfast bowl. Top with strawberries and spoon over the 'whipped cream'. (The three very different textures in this breakfast idea create an interesting as well as tasty combination.)

spinach and mushroom on toast

serves 2

300g mushrooms, peeled and
  cleaned
½ cup water
¼ cup skim milk
2 tbsps cornflour

4 spinach/silver beet (white stalks
  removed) leaves
low fat cottage cheese
2 thick slices of wholemeal toast

Place mushrooms and water in a saucepan. Leave on lowest heat setting for 1 hour to gently simmer. Make a paste with the milk and cornflour. Stir through mushrooms to thicken. Cook for further 2 minutes. Turn off heat and leave lid on. Steam spinach leaves for 2 minutes. Drain.

Spread toast with cottage cheese, 2 spinach leaves per slice of toast and spoon over mushrooms. Serve.

Note: mushrooms can be cooked the night before and reheated in the morning.

wholemeal toast with spreads

Lightly toast your favourite bread (wholemeal, rye or sourdough, suitable salt free, sugar free, oil free and preservative free varieties). Choose from any of the spreads (see Spreads Section) or arrange two or three different varieties in small containers.

a barbecue

The concept of a barbecue is an excellent way to entertain friends in a casual fashion. However, many a barbecue has become the inevitable menu of 'steaks, a tossed salad and a coleslaw with bread and butter'.

Here are some rather untypical barbecue suggestions. The quantities aren't important, as a barbecue can range from 2 to 200 people. What food and how to present it, how to create a sumptuous meal that's good for you is by far the most important thing.

Along with the following recipes serve baskets of hot wholemeal breads and rolls and plenty of baskets of fresh fruit.

You may like to let your guests do the work by simply providing the food and the foil and let them put their own combinations together.

baked apples

Core an apple. Fill with dried fruits, shake of cinnamon. Pour over some fruit juice. Wrap securely in foil. Place in glowing coals for 15–20 minutes or until soft when skewered.

baked bananas

Rub the outside of the bananas with oil and place them directly on coals. When the skins turn black the bananas are cooked. Open and top with non-fat natural yoghurt. Serve immediately.

baked potatoes

Allow 1 or 2 large potatoes per person. Wash skin thoroughly. Wrap in foil, sprinkle over some herbs, seal, cook over glowing coals for about 1 to 1¼ hours, or try some of these suggestions.

Cut a V shaped cavity in top of potato and fill with any of the following and seal and cook as above.

Fillings:

- Strip of low fat grating cheese and 2 tablespoons of chopped spring onions, dash of paprika.
- Two tablespoons of low fat cottage cheese and 2 tablespoons of fresh chopped herbs.
- Two tablespoons of low fat cottage cheese, some grated carrot and finely chopped red pepper.
- Fill cavity with cooked apple, sprinkle over with cinnamon and a good squeeze of lemon juice.

baked tomatoes

Place a large tomato on a sheet of foil. Throw over herbs (oregano and basil blend well with tomatoes) and some chopped shallots. Seal foil. Either place in glowing coals for about 10 minutes or place on top of barbecue.

banana-rama whole fish

1 whole fish on foil

Slice a banana or two and 6 fresh apricots over the fish. Add 1 tablespoon of capers. Pour over 1 cup of unsweetened orange juice. Seal and place on the barbecue.

(See fish varieties in Ingredients section.)

beef kebabs

Choose prime rump beef and remove all visible fat. Cut steak into 3cm square pieces. Allow 2 squares per person. Marinate the meat in a suitable marinade for about 3–4 hours or overnight and drain before threading onto skewers.

Marinade Suggestions:

Yoghurt Marinade

1 cup non-fat natural yoghurt
2 cloves garlic crushed
1 teaspoon curry powder
1 tbsp unsweetened orange juice

Spicy Marinade

1/2 cup dry white wine/apple juice
1 clove garlic crushed
2 tbsps low salt soy sauce

1 tbsp lemon juice
1 tbsp apple cider vinegar

To prepare kebabs, on each skewer place 1 whole mushroom, 1 piece of beef, 1 chunk of onion, 1 chunk of pineapple, another piece of meat, pineapple and onion, finish with a mushroom.

Variation:
Piece of capsicum, piece of pineapple, meat, 2 cherry tomatoes, meat, pineapple and finish with capsicum.

Using a basting brush wipe kebabs with remaining marinade and place on the barbecue (make sure flame is low). Cook for 10–15 minutes turning as they cook.

garlic whole schnapper

1 whole schnapper
Rub fish all over with lemon juice and the inside. Crush 3–4 cloves of garlic into 1/4 cup non-fat natural yoghurt. Using a basting brush, wipe yoghurt garlic mixture over fish. Sit fish on lettuce leaves on foil. Sprinkle over fresh dill and pour over 1/4 cup dry white wine. Seal and place on barbecue.

grapefruit grill

Cut grapefruit in half. Cut into segments (do not remove from the grapefruit shell). Place a piece of foil on top of the barbecue grill or hot plate. Place the grapefruit flesh side down and leave for 10–15 minutes or until the grapefruit is hot. Serve.

hot fruit salad

Remove the top from a grapefruit. Scoop out flesh and remove pith, segment the fruit and chop up. Combine with any other fruits in season, such as oranges, pineapple, bananas, strawberries, apples, kiwi fruit, peaches, apricots, berries. (Chop all fruit roughly). Pour a small amount of unsweetened fruit juice and 1 teaspoon of brandy in the bottom of the grapefruit shell. Pile in as much fruit as possible. Sit grapefruit shell in foil so it will stand upright. Place on barbecue for approximately 15 minutes. Serve immediately, with 'whipped cream' (see recipe Banana Date Steamed Pudding in Special Occasions Desserts section).

potato salad

Use small potatoes. Remove skins and lightly steam. Add fresh herbs (parsley, chives, dill), mint and some chopped odourless onion. (Steamed potatoes don't need dressing as the moisture is still in them.) Use ¼ cup mayonnaise if necessary.

rice and capsicum salad

Cooked brown rice. Red and green capsicum cut into fine slithers.

Yoghurt Dressing:

1 cup non-fat natural yoghurt	¼ teaspoon paprika
2 teaspoons cider vinegar	1 teaspoon finely grated lemon rind

Line a salad bowl with broken lettuce leaves. Line the lettuce leaves with slices of cucumber and apple rings and fill the centre with rice and slithers of capsicums. Pour over dressing.

tomato, orange and onion salad

Remove skin and pith from oranges, cut into round slices, cut tomatoes into round slices, cut onion into rings. Combine in a salad bowl. Pour over cider vinegar and freshly chopped mint. Chill before serving.

vegetable and fruit kebabs

Thread suitable vegetable and fruit chunks on a skewer. Place on a large sheet of foil. Pour over liquid and seal. Cook approximately 5–15 minutes depending on vegetables and fruits used.

- zucchini, cauliflower, capsicum, mushroom (repeat)
- brussel sprouts, celery chunks, (repeat)
- zucchini, cherry tomatoes (repeat)
- pineapple chunks, apple chunks (repeat) (sprinkle with cinnamon)
- banana chunks, pineapple chunks, (repeat) squeeze over lemon juice
- orange chunks, zucchini, onions (repeat)
- baby squash, small onions (repeat)

If using wooden skewers thread vegetables and fruit on skewer and immerse in water or fruit juice for a few minutes before barbecuing. This means the skewers won't burn.

vegetable combination

Clean the top of a barbecue hot plate. You will need a cup of vegetable or other stock or add 2 crushed cloves of garlic to a cup of water. Allow about 500g fresh chopped vegetables for 4 people.

Suitable vegetables to use are onions, carrots, beans, potatoes, sweet potatoes, capsicum, mushrooms, celery, zucchini, bean shoots, cauliflower, baby squash. Cut vegetables into even bite sized pieces (either finely slice or cut into julienne strips).

Pour a small amount of stock onto hot plate and quickly add onions. Use an egg lifter to keep them moving so they don't stick or burn (don't have hot plate too hot). Add other vegetables and stock as needed so vegetables do not dry out. Cook for 3–5 minutes and serve immediately. Sprinkle over your favourite herbs if desired.

whole fish barbecued

Choose those fish low in oil. Clean thoroughly and leave whole fish intact. Lay fish on a large piece of foil and place on barbecue. Seal foil. Remember that fish takes very little cooking. Keep an eye on them – when flesh is white and breaks away easily, it is cooked. Try squeezing over lemon juice, unsweetened orange juice or vegetable stock and sprinkle over herbs of your choice.

whole fish with shallots

1 whole fish on foil

Cut 5 slits across fish and gently ease open. Squeeze lemon juice into each slit. Cut thin strips of low fat grating cheese to fit in each slit and place 2 cleaned and peeled shallots on top of cheese in each split. Sprinkle over plenty of fresh parsley and 1 cup of apple juice. Seal and place on barbecue.

summer sunday

Summer Sundays can be a very refreshing day off! It is great to spend a Sunday, just nibbling at fresh food all day and doing all those things you've been putting off, or having a lovely quiet day with the family or restoring the garden after the weeds have made their presence felt.

A lazy Summer Sunday needs just a little work to make it all come together, but it is worth it for then the whole day is yours.

apple and cucumber in vinaigrette

serves 10–12

6 large jonathan or granny smith
　apples
½ cup lemon juice
4 cucumbers

100g small mushrooms
1 cup vinaigrette (I prefer garlic
　vinaigrette)

Core apples. Cut into thin julienne strips. Soak in lemon juice, stirring frequently. Peel cucumbers, cut in half and remove seeds. Slice into half rounds. Thoroughly wash and drain mushrooms. Cut in half. Combine all ingredients and toss well. Refrigerate.

baby beets in orange curried sauce

serves 10–12

40 small or 20 medium beetroot
1–2 quantities of orange curried
　sauce (see Dressings section)

Lightly steam beetroot until tender. Peel. If using medium size beetroot, cut in half or quarters. Place in serving bowl. Pour over dressing. Cover and refrigerate.

153

kiwi fruit

serves 10–12
12 kiwi fruit

Peel fruit. Leave whole or cut into slices.
Place in serving bowl and chill.

lemon mineral water

serves 10–12
ice blocks
2 lemons

mineral water (low sodium, natural), 285ml per person.

Place ice blocks in a large jug. Cut lemons into thin round slices, and put in jug. Pour over mineral water.
   Garnish each glass with sprigs of mint.

pineapple

serves 10–12
2 large pineapples

Peel and remove core. Cut into chunks. Place in serving bowl and chill.

potatoes in spicy tomato dressing

serves 10–12
40 small new potatoes
1 quantity spicy tomato dressing
   (see Dressings section)

Wash potatoes and peel if necessary. Lightly steam until just tender. Rinse in cold water and drain thoroughly. Place in serving bowl. Pour over dressing. Cover and refrigerate.

strawberries

serves 10–12
1 kg strawberries

Wash and drain well. Place in serving bowl and chill.

tomato and capsicum strips with herbs

serves 10–12

6 medium tomatoes
2 red capsicums
2 green capsicums
1 cup finely chopped mixed herbs
    (chives, parsley, oregano, basil,
    rosemary etc.)

¼ cup lemon or unsweetened
    grapefruit juice.

Cut tomatoes in half. Scoop out seeds and flesh. Cut tomato into thin strips. Cut capsicums in half. Remove stalk and seeds. Cut into thin strips. Combine all ingredients and toss well. Refrigerate.

tossed lettuce, beans and sprouts

serves 10–12

1 large lettuce (any variety)
4 cups cut and cooked french beans
2 cups sprouts (alfalfa, mung or
    lentil)

1 cup grated baby carrots
½ cup grated small parsnip

Break lettuce into small pieces. Soak in chilled water for 10 minutes. Drain well. Combine all ingredients and toss well. Cover and refrigerate.

it's child's play

a birthday party

A child's birthday party or just a gathering of young friends is an excellent opportunity to encourage children to eat sensibly, with just a few treats. Just as children dress up for their special occasion, let's dress up the every day fruits and vegetables they eat on a well dressed table of brilliant colours. With fruits and vegetables you can create an activity that all children will enjoy and eat the final product. The main rule is that all children have very clean hands (provide a container of hot soapy water and towels).

If you don't have children in your household, don't ignore this section — relive your childhood instead. You might discover a favourite dish among these ideas.

a parting gift

Buy some 40cm garden stakes at a nursery (a few pence each). To each stake, tie a balloon, party whistle, special pencil (or other small treat) and in clear cellophane wrap some dried fruits; (apricots, sultanas etc.) and fasten with a colourful tie.

apple muffins

makes approximately 12

1½ cups self raising wholemeal
   flour
¼ teaspoon mixed spice
½ teaspoon cinnamon
½ cup sultanas
2 egg whites
½ cup skim milk

2 tbsps cold compressed almond oil
   (available at health food shops)
1 cup roughly chopped cooked
   apple
1 tbsp pure maple syrup or apple
   juice concentrate

Sift flour, spices and add sultanas. Beat egg whites and add oil, apple, maple syrup and skim milk. Blend thoroughly. Add to the dry ingredients and stir until thoroughly mixed. Turn into a lightly greased muffin tin and bake in a moderately hot oven for 15–20 minutes or until cooked.

Serve hot from the oven.

birthday cake

Cover a small box with coloured paper. Stick the appropriate number of candles along the top of the box. Place box in the centre of a tray. Scatter all around with lots of crushed and cubed ice. Place enough popsicles around in the ice for each child. Light the candles – 'Happy Birthday'.

carrot curls

Using a peeler, peel down the length of carrot from top to bottom to make long strips. Place in a container of water and place in the refrigerator for several hours. Carrot strips will curl up. Drain before serving.

Use as a garnish for raisin and carrot triangles.

drinks

Freshly squeezed fruit juices, for example, orange, orange and lemon, apple, pineapple.

Serve jugs of chilled water with lots of cut fresh fruit and sprigs of mint. Suitable fruit to use would be slices of oranges and lemons, strawberries, pineapple chunks, grapes etc.

Serve drinks with straws and bows attached.

floating boats

makes 1
1 banana
a triangle of watermelon (3cm
    thick)

Peel the banana. Cut off the ends. Quickly dip into lemon juice to coat. Cut a small slice off the bottom of the banana so it stands by itself. Use a piece of wooden skewer to place the watermelon sail in the centre of banana. Freeze for 1 hour before serving.

fruit popsicles

Grape Delight: Fill a plastic icy-pole maker with green grapes. Top up with dark unsweetened grape juice. Cut out a coloured cardboard circle and put a hole in the centre to insert stick through. Freeze.

Banana: Mash bananas and squeeze over with lemon juice. Push into icy-pole maker. Cover with a small white doily and insert stick through. Freeze.

Pineapple Crunch: Fill icy-pole maker with finely chopped fresh pineapple. Juice remaining pineapple or use unsweetened orange juice to top up each icy-pole. Insert stick and freeze.

Strawberry Crèmes: Combine equal quantities of fresh hulled strawberries and non-fat natural yoghurt. Purée and pour into icy-pole maker. Insert stick and freeze.

making a face

Provide each child with a large white paper plate, a cutting board and small knife (if children are too small for knives, cut up all ingredients in different shapes).

In the centre of the table, have large bowls of shredded lettuce, alfalfa sprouts, cherry tomatoes, cucumber rings, carrot strips, celery pieces, green beans, shelled peas, and apple chunks.

Now sit down with the children and start them off by giving them an example of how to make a face using the ingredients. When everyone is finished – now let's eat it, nose first and so on. (Don't be frightened to sit down and eat your creation with the children.)

making an animal

Provide the children with one whole fruit or vegetable, toothpicks, a small knife and cutting board. Suggestions for the whole fruit or vegetable are: orange, apple, pear, lemon, carrot, capsicum.

In the centre of the table have large bowls of grapes, cherries, cherry tomatoes, banana chunks, dried apricots, sultanas, strawberries, apricot halves, peaches cut into cubes, carrot strips, celery chunks, cubes of orange.

The animal need not be realistic. Suggest to the children that it may have more than 4 legs, 2 heads, a long tail, floppy ears, a long nose etc.

When animals are completed let each child give their animal a name before they eat it.

orange butterflies

Cut oranges into quarters. Freeze until hard. Remove just before serving. Use an 8cm piece of celery or carrot as the body of the butterfly. Use a wooden skewer to thread through 1 orange quarter on either side of the body.

party sausages

makes 2 dozen party size or 14 long

1 kg peeled potatoes
350–400g grated vegetables (for example, 1 cup cooked peas, ½ cup grated carrot, 2 tbsps finely chopped shallots, grated capsicum, 2 small zucchini grated).

2 cups fine wholemeal breadcrumbs
50g finely grated low fat grating cheese

Cook potatoes until tender. Drain and mash. Add vegetables, breadcrumbs and cheese, while potato is still warm. Mix thoroughly. Shape into sausages of desired length. Place under griller and turn to brown and crisp up the outside of sausages (turn carefully). Serve with tomato sauce.

pumpkin muffins

Working from the recipe for Apple Muffins in this section, substitute 1 cup cold cooked and mashed pumpkin for apple, ½ cup currants for sultanas, and ½ teaspoon nutmeg for cinnamon.

raisin and carrot triangles

wholemeal bread slices
grated baby carrots

finely minced raisins
low fat ricotta cheese

Lightly spread bread with ricotta cheese. Combine carrot and raisins and mix well. Spread over bread. Top with another slice of bread. Continue until all bread and mixture is used. Stack on top of each other. Even up by removing crusts. Cut into triangles. Arrange on plate with carrot curls to garnish.

sausage rolls

makes 24
½ quantity of party sausage mixture   4 sheets of wholemeal filo pastry.
   (see recipe in this section)

Take 2 sheets of pastry, one on top of the other. On the nearest edge of the pastry place a line of filling. Gently roll up the filling in the pastry. Place on a non-stick oven tray. Use a sharp knife to cut through sausage roll about every 4cm, but do not separate. Repeat with remaining pastry and mixture. Wipe tops lightly with beaten egg white and sprinkle over with poppy seeds. Cook in a hot oven 200°C for 20 minutes, or until browned. Serve with tomato sauce.

stick dolls

makes 1

1 wooden skewer
1 small white paper doily
½ apple
4cm piece of banana

1 stick of carrot
1 small fresh apricot
2 sultanas

Attach doily to wooden skewer to form a skirt about ¼ of the way up the skewer, push ½ apple down to rest on top of doily, then banana. Push carrot horizontally onto skewer in the centre of the stick of carrot. Carefully remove stone from apricot without breaking apricot in two. Push apricot on to skewer last. Use toothpick pieces to put 2 sultana eyes on the apricot. Halve oranges, grapefruits, or melons and use to hold stick dolls. Place on a plate for the table.

tomato sauce

makes approximately 3 litres

3kg ripe tomatoes, peeled and seeds
    removed
2 large onions, chopped finely
3 large granny smith apples, peeled
    and chopped
2 large carrots, grated

300ml vinegar
300ml water
½ teaspoon mace
⅛ teaspoon ground cloves
¼ teaspoon cayenne pepper

Combine all ingredients in a large saucepan and bring to the boil. Then simmer uncovered for 1 to 1½ hours or until sauce is thick, stirring occasionally. Remove from heat. Purée in a food processor. Pour into bottles. Cool. Keep in refrigerator.

christmas dinner

Christmas in our home will always be a very special occasion: the emphasis being to gather as many family members together as possible. It is a time of exchanging small gifts bought with much love – nibbling food as we go.

More and more I see it as a day where the company is more important than the food we eat. The hostess should not have to slave over a hot stove the get the traditional 'hot' Christmas Dinner on the table. Keep the food which is served simple, and if food can be prepared in advance, all the better.

It is a day to indulge just a little – but not too much!

Select a choice from the menu or a little everything.

Recipes on the Christmas menu are:

Platter of Fresh Fruits

or

Platter of Fresh Raw Vegetables served with Cheese Logs or Cheese Fruit Balls

Asparagus Mousse

or

Curried Scallops served on a bed of Brown Rice

Chicken Terrine (hot) served with Blueberry Sauce and Vegetables: baked potato, bean parcels, and a baked herb tomato.

or

Breast of Turkey (hot) seved with Orange Curry Sauce, Wild Rice and Festive Salad.

Cold Christmas Pudding served with Vanilla Crème

or

Apricot and Passionfruit Cheesecake

or

Layered Salad of Fruits

163

platter of fresh fruits

Fruit is ideal to start any meal, as it is a cleanser of the palate and light enough not to spoil the appetite for later.

On a large platter arrange a variety of fruits all in bite size pieces.

Select from: apricots, cherries, mango, gooseberries, mulberries, papaw, peaches, pineapple, kiwi fruit (Chinese gooseberries), plums, strawberries, raspberries, loganberries, bananas, grapes, watermelon.

platter of fresh raw vegetables

Like fruits, vegetables will cleanse the palate in preparation for what is to come without being too filling.

On a large platter arrange a selection of colourful bite size vegetables. Vary the shapes, cut differently or soak some in iced water to curl.

Select from:

carrot curls – using a peeler, peel down the length of the carrot and place in a large bowl of iced water to curl.

carrot crackers – using a sharp knife cut down the length of the carrot from top to bottom about ¼cm thick. Cut into 4cm to 6cm rounds and place in a large bowl of iced water to crisp.

radishes – if they are small, simply clean, remove tail; if they are large, cut them in half or with a sharp knife, cut 6 small slits, at the top of the radish. Soak in iced water until the top pieces separate and flute out.

snow peas – top and tail.

button mushrooms – wash thoroughly.

cherry tomatoes – wash thoroughly.

capsicum strips – cut long, thin strips of red and green capsicum.

cauliflower flowerettes – choose very white, firm heads and break off in bite size pieces. Blanch in boiling water for 1 minute. Drain and drop into cold water. Drain.

cucumber rounds – wash the outside of the cucumber thoroughly. Cut into ½cm rounds.

spring onions – remove roots on the shallot and peel away the outside layer of skin. Cut away rough green end leaving about 6cm of green to work with. Using a very sharp knife or pair of scissors cut as many slits as possible in the green part of the shallot. Soak in iced water until the green part curls up tightly. Drain well.

broccoli flowerettes – choose firm headed flowerettes with a 3cm stem (approximately). Blanch in boiling water for 1 minute. Drain and drop into cold water. Drain.

celery chunks – cut celery stalks about 4cm long on the diagonal.

cheese logs

serves 12

1 cup low fat ricotta cheese
1 cup non-fat cottage cheese
¼ cup finely chopped chives
2 tbsps finely grated carrot
2 tbsps finely chopped celery
2 tbsps finely chopped red
  capsicum

2 teaspoons finely grated lemon
  rind *or*
1 teaspoon dried sage
poppy seeds

Mix all ingredients except poppy seeds thoroughly together with a fork. Shape into a log and chill, wrap in foil. Before serving, roll in poppy seeds.

Serve with vegetables or cut out rounds or triangles of wholemeal bread and toast under griller or in the oven until browned and crisp. Leave to cool.

cheese fruit balls

makes 12 large
24 small

1 cup low fat ricotta cheese
1 cup non-fat cottage cheese
¼ cup sultanas
2 tbsps finely chopped raisins
2 tbsps finely chopped apricots

2 tbsps finely chopped, well drained
  unsweetened pineapple
pulp of one passionfruit (optional)
finely chopped parsley, or lemon
  balm

Mix all ingredients together thoroughly with a fork. Roll into small balls, roll in parsley or lemon balm and chill.

asparagus mousse

serves 10

700g asparagus, cooked
1¼ cups liquid that asparagus has been cooked in
1 tbsp onion, finely grated
2½ level tbsps gelatine

½ cup hot liquid (made up of 2 tbsps lemon juice and the rest, boiling water)
1¼ cups non-fat natural yoghurt
4 egg whites

Place asparagus, 1¼ cups asparagus liquid and onion in a food processor and blend until smooth. Pour ½ cup hot liquid over gelatine and mix until gelatine is dissolved. Turn food processor on and add gelatine. Place food processor bowl in the refrigerator until mixture starts to set around the edge. Return to food processor and add yoghurt.

Beat egg whites and fold through asparagus mixture. Pour into individual moulds or one large one. Refrigerate for at least 4 hours.

Garnish with thin strips or slices of vegetables, carrot curls and thinly sliced cucumber.

curried scallops

serves 12
36–40 scallops

Curry Sauce

1 clove garlic crushed
1 medium onion, finely chopped
½ cup celery, finely chopped
1 tbsp wholemeal plain flour
1–1½ tbsp curry powder
2½ cups (fat free) chicken stock

3 tbsps tomato paste, salt free
½ cup cooked apple purée
1 tbsp lemon juice
2 tbsps finely chopped parsley
½–1 cup non-fat yoghurt (optional)

Sauté garlic and onion in tablespoon of water until soft. Add celery, stir in wholemeal flour and curry powder and cook for 3 minutes, stirring continually. Add chicken stock, tomato paste, apple purée and lemon juice. Cover and simmer for 30 minutes, stirring frequently. Add parsley.

May be stored in the refrigerator for use when required. It will keep for 1 week.

If a milder curry is required, add non-fat yoghurt just prior to serving.

chicken terrine (hot)

serves 10–12

1kg chicken fillets, minced
3 cups wholemeal breadcrumbs
4 granny smith apples, grated
¾ cup chopped spring onions

2 teaspoons finely grated lemon
  rind
1 egg white

Mix all ingredients thoroughly with your hands. Press firmly into a foil lined large terrine. Cook in a water bath at 200°C for 1½ hours. Turn out onto a serving dish. Place vegetables around it. Serve with Blueberry Sauce (see next recipe).

blueberry sauce

½ cup blueberry conserve
1 cup unsweetened apple juice

1 tbsp arrowroot

Combine blueberry conserve with apple juice and stir well. Bring to a gentle simmer. Mix arrowroot with a small amount of water and add to the blueberries and apple juice. Stir until thick. Remove from heat. Allow 1–2 tablespoons of blueberry sauce per person.

vegetables
baked potatoes

Allow 2 medium potatoes per person. Peel. Cut approximately 10 slits with a sharp knife across the top of the potato in diagonal lines. Place all the potatoes in a large oven bag, cut side up. Seal bag. Prick 2 or 3 holes in bag. Place in oven at 200°C and cook until potatoes are golden brown.

bean parcels

Allow approximately 12 whole beans per person. Remove ends and remove any strings. Cut fine strips of the green part of a leek. Use these to tie beans into bundles. Place in a steamer. Cook until tender, but not overcooked.

baked herb tomato

Allow 1 medium tomato per person. Wash thoroughly. Cut a slit in top of tomato. Gently ease apart and sprinkle in herbs of your choice: for example, parsley, chives, oregano, basil or rosemary. Place a small square of wholemeal bread on top of each tomato. Sprinkle over with 1 teaspoon of finely grated low fat grating cheese. Cook in a hot oven until tomato is heated through and bread and cheese are well browned.

breast of turkey with orange curry sauce

1 × 1kg turkey breast (remove skin and visible fat)
1 onion
2 granny smith apples

2 teaspoons finely grated orange rind
1 teaspoon dried sage
1 teaspoon dried thyme
1 cup dry white wine/water

Lightly pound the turkey breast. Peel and slice the onion and the apples. Place onion and apple slices on the bottom of a shallow baking pan. Place the turkey breast on top of the onion and apple. Sprinkle over orange rind, sage, thyme, and pour over white wine/water. Cover. Cook at 190°C for 2 hours. Meat is cooked when you insert a fine skewer through meat and juices are clear.

Let turkey stand for a few minutes before slicing. Use an electric knife to cut into 10 to 12 portions. Keep hot. Serve with Orange Curry Sauce (see Dressings section).

wild rice

(Expensive! but an interesting once a year taste experience.) Cook as per instructions on the packet.

festive salad

per person
4 small asparagus spears
½ medium beetroot
½ cup tarragon vinegar
4 segments of cantaloup

small bunch green grapes
3 snow peas
½ small lemon

Steam asparagus just lightly. It should be still slightly crisp. Cut off ends. Peel the beetroot. Simmer in enough water to just cover and add ½ cup tarragon vinegar. Cook until beetroot are tender. Drain. Cool and refrigerate. Slice cantaloup into small segments (like the shape of an orange segment). Wash the grapes. Cook snow peas for 2 to 3 minutes and plunge in cold water. Drain. Arrange salad on individual plates. Squeeze lemon juice over asparagus.

cold christmas pudding

serves 10–12

125g sultanas
125g dried apricots, finely chopped
125g prunes, chopped
125g currants
1 cup unsweetened orange juice
1 teaspoon mixed spice

2 tbsps dry sherry
425g cold cooked apple
1 tbsp lemon juice
½ cup unsweetened apple juice
2 tbsps gelatine
¼ cup boiling water

Combine fruit, orange juice, mixed spice and sherry in a saucepan. Slowly bring to the boil. Simmer for 3 minutes. Remove from heat. Fold through apple. Combine lemon juice and apple juice. Dissolve gelatine in boiling water and add to apple and lemon juice. Pour over fruit and apple mixture and mix well. Spoon into a 6 cup capacity pudding mould.

Cover and refrigerate overnight or longer. Use a sharp knife to slice into portions.

vanilla crème

1 cup low fat ricotta cheese
¾ cup unsweetened apple juice

1–2 teaspoons vanilla essence
2 teaspoons brandy

Whip all ingredients in a blender until smooth and chill.

apricot and passionfruit cheesecake

serves 12

Base:

1 cup wholemeal breadcrumbs
¼ cup whole almonds in their skins
2 tbsps rolled oats

1 teaspoon almond essence (pure extract)
1 egg white

Filling:

250g non-fat cottage cheese
250g low fat ricotta cheese
2 tbsps unsweetened orange juice
2 tbsps lemon juice
1 teaspoon vanilla essence

1 tbsp gelatine
⅓ cup boiling water
1 cup non-fat yoghurt
2 egg whites

Topping:

435g cooked apricots

pulp of 3 passionfruit

To make base:

Combine all the base ingredients except the egg white in a food processor and process for 2 minutes. Add the egg white. Process until all egg white is absorbed. Lightly grease a cheesecake spring form tin. Press crumb mixture firmly onto the base. Cook at 200°C for 10 minutes. Remove and cool.

To make filling:

Combine cottage cheese, ricotta cheese, orange juice, lemon juice and vanilla in a food processor and blend until smooth. Dissolve gelatine in boiling water. Let cool slightly. Add to cheese mixture and blend through. Add yoghurt and blend through. Beat egg whites until stiff and gently fold through cheese mixture. Pour over base and refrigerate for at least 2 hours.

To arrange topping:

When cheesecake is set, place the apricots around the edge of the cheesecake. Spoon over passionfruit pulp. Return cheesecake to the refrigerator.

The cheesecake is at its best after being refrigerated for 48 hours.

Variation:

Substitute preserved peaches for apricots (see Home Preserves section)

layered salad of fruits

Choose a large glass bowl for best effect

fruit of your choice, at least 6
   varieties

1 cup passionfruit pulp
½ glass champagne (optional)

Create a layered effect by placing one fruit on top of the other. Try this combination:

Begin with strawberries
top with thin slices of pineapple
top with cubes of papaw
top with green grapes/purple grapes
top with thin slices of nectarine
top with thin slices of kiwi fruit
top with thin strips of peach

Pour over 1 cup of passionfruit pulp and ½ glass champagne (only for this special occasion, and optional).

The quantity of fruit used will depend on your choice of bowl. You will become familiar with the quantity it holds and how many it serves. However, don't worry if you have too much – you can never have enough fresh fruit salad on hand, and the flavours in this improve as it stands.

christmas cake

This is an adaptation of the Fruity Pumpkin Cake in *Taste of Life*. It is a much larger cake (approximately 2kg) and the dash of brandy and variety of dried fruits makes it an excellent choice for the Christmas Cake.

125g dried apricots
125g raisins
125g mixed dried peel
125g currants
250g prunes
250g dates
2 tbsps brandy and/or unsweetened
   orange juice to make 1 cup
   liquid
60g almonds in their skins
   (optional)

2 cups mashed pumpkin
½ cup apple juice concentrate
4 cups wholemeal plain flour
4 teaspoons baking powder
2 teaspoons baking soda
1 teaspoon cinnamon
1 teaspoon mixed spice
½ teaspoon nutmeg
6 egg whites
1 tbsp vanilla essence

Chop fruits and soak in brandy and orange juice, covered, overnight. Roughly chop almonds and add to the fruit. Add pumpkin and apple juice concentrate. Mix well. Sift all the dry ingredients, twice. Fold flour into the fruit mixture in three lots and mix well. Beat egg whites until stiff. Gently fold egg whites through cake mixture. Add vanilla essence.

Prepare a 23cm × 7cm deep round cake tin with foil or non-stick baking paper. Cut a long strip of brown paper approximately 10 cm width. Secure it around the top of the tin so that approximately 7cm of brown paper is above the tin. Pour cake mixture into tin and spread evenly. Decorate with whole almonds if desired.

Cook at 170°C for 2½–3 hours. Test after 2½ hours with a fine skewer. Remove from oven. Cover with brown paper and tea towels to keep the moisture in the cake. When cool, wrap in foil or plastic and keep in sealed container.

index

176